Guided MATH

A Framework for Mathematics Instruction

Author

Laney Sammons

Foreword by Janis K. Fackler, Ph.D.

SHELL EDUCATION

Guided Math

Editors
Sara Johnson
Kristy Stark M.A.Ed

Editorial Director
Lori Kamola, M.S.Ed.

Editor-in-Chief
Sharon Coan, M.S.Ed.

Editorial Manager
Gisela Lee

Creative Director
Lee Aucoin

Print Production Manager
Don Tran

Interior Layout Designer
Robin Erickson

Publisher
Corinne Burton, M.A.Ed.

The names in this book have been changed to protect the identities of teachers and students.

The photos in this book were taken by Wendy Hamm.

Shell Education
5301 Oceanus Drive
Huntington Beach, CA 92649-1030
http://www.shelleducation.com
ISBN 978-1-4258-0534-0
© 2010 Shell Educational Publishing, Inc.
Reprinted 2013

The classroom teacher may reproduce copies of materials in this book for classroom use only. The reproduction of any part for an entire school or school system is strictly prohibited. No part of this publication may be transmitted, stored, or recorded in any form without written permission from the publisher.

Table of Contents

Table of Contents *(cont.)*

Table of Contents (cont.)

Foreword

A Mathematical Perspective

Today, we live in a time of extraordinary and accelerating change, and the need to understand and be able to use mathematics in everyday life has never been greater. Mathematics education has gone through many changes. It has progressed from a static field of study to a dynamic status. Demands of the new century require that all children acquire an understanding of mathematical concepts, proficiency in skills, and positive attitudes towards mathematics (National Council of Teachers of Mathematics 2000). In 2001, with the federal *No Child Left Behind Act* being enacted, steps were taken to ensure that all children met rigorous academic standards. Each state increased what they expected from the students, which in turn has placed far more pressure on the teachers.

Computation and drill have dominated the curriculum for a long time, but in this century, new approaches of instruction are necessary in order to help students understand and appreciate mathematics. The belief that people understand the meanings of the mathematical procedures they have learned to perform is a fallacy. Indeed, many people perform mathematical calculations without understanding the underlying principles or meanings. Symbols and rules have very little to do with their intuitions, their ideas of what makes sense, or their conceptual understanding (Heibert and Carpenter 1992). Teaching that focuses on procedural skills, or skills in isolation, causes students to see mathematics as boring and difficult, which is very destructive.

When first introduced to this book I was very skeptical. I thought, 'Oh no, someone else has come up with another plan to take the joy out of learning mathematics.' I assumed that the author used the word *guided* as a way to spoon-feed children the mathematics in a very robotic approach, not taking into consideration that the mathematics strands need to be intertwined and not always taught in isolation. Not to mention that mathematics should be fun and exciting as

7

connections arc discovered and the beauty of it is exposed. We are all living in a time of accountability, where everything seems to be very prescriptive with each math topic being taught in isolation. So many programs lose the big picture, but not this one.

My first impression was very wrong! This author sees the big picture and has managed to find the right formula to teaching mathematics to meet the needs of all the learners, by, as she states it, "guiding, prodding, and piquing the curiosity of her learners." Connections are always made to previous lessons and to the real world as the students are kept actively engaged. Opinions and ideas are not only allowed to be voiced, but valued during the Math Huddle. The classroom is drenched in numeracy, mathematical terminology, and mathematical thinking. This environment, rich in mathematical opportunities, is very important. It affects and promotes students' ability to effectively develop personal control over their mathematical knowledge.

The most important feature of learning with understanding is that it is generative; that is, when students acquire knowledge with understanding, they can apply that knowledge to learn new topics and solve unfamiliar problems. When these ideas or processes are not learned with understanding, each new topic is perceived as an isolated skill, and skills cannot be applied to solve problems that are not explicitly taught. For learning to be generative, knowledge must be acquired in ways that clarify how that knowledge can be used. Students must be engaged in learning that involves the same generative process in order to apply it to learn new ideas and solve unfamiliar problems for the future (Franke et al. 2001). It is my belief that the learning that will take place by using the Guided Math approach suggested, is the learning that we would all want our students to have: learning for understanding.

Janis K. Drab Fackler
contributing author of *Strategies for Teaching Mathematics*

Preface

Without a doubt, most people join the teaching profession because they care deeply about our young people and place great value on education. I am no exception. In 1989, when my younger child entered first grade, I tentatively entered a kindergarten classroom as a rookie teacher. I don't know who was more nervous—the eighteen youngsters who were beginning school for the first time or me.

The vast differences between my students became apparent to me very quickly. One of my students did not know what crayons were. She had never held a pencil before. Several children had attended a preschool that focused on traditional kindergarten skills. They knew their numbers through ten and could write their names and several sight words beautifully. Another child, before he had even put his jacket in his cubby, curled up on the floor in deep slumber. Some children had a strong sense of story and loved listening to read alouds. Others were unable to follow and comprehend simple stories. A few students had difficulty getting along with their peers. Almost all of them struggled initially with the idea of doing things together as a class rather than following their individual interests. As I led lessons and tried to establish smooth transitions, it often felt as if I were trying to carry a load of laundry. One sock would fall to the floor and as I picked it up, another would drop. And, so it was with my students. Just as one student was coaxed back into the group, another would head off to pursue something that had just attracted his or her attention.

The differences I observed in my kindergarten class that year are mirrored in classrooms throughout the country in elementary, middle, and high schools. Fortunately for me, in my classroom, there was a very talented and experienced full-time teaching assistant. Just as she was able to provide support and scaffolding for me as a rookie teacher, she and I were able to do the same for my "rookie" students. By working with my students in small groups and differentiating instruction for them, all of these students were eventually successful and ready to move on to the first grade.

I've often heard the expression "Everything I need to know for life I learned in kindergarten." I might change that slightly to say "everything I need to know *to teach* I learned in kindergarten." My years of teaching kindergarten taught me how important it is to find out all you possibly can about your students and then to adjust your instruction to meet their ever-changing needs. Rather than becoming frustrated teaching one-size-fits-all lessons, my teaching assistant and I spent lots of time supporting struggling learners, prodding reluctant learners, piquing the curiosity of adventurous learners and, with all, praising their accomplishments as we guided them toward the next steps of their learning.

In the ensuing years, I moved to other schools and grade levels. Although the needs of the students in each grade I taught were as diverse as those in my first kindergarten class, the support of a full-time teaching assistant was no longer available. I faced the daunting task of trying to help those students achieve academic success while recognizing that they each had unique needs. Whole-class instruction made this very difficult. I had a vision of how student needs could be met with a teaching assistant in the classroom. How could I adapt that vision to make it feasible to implement in my classroom without any assistance? Moreover, my colleagues were facing the same challenges. Together, we devised plans for working with small groups of students while the rest of the class was engaged in independent work. Unit pretesting gave us an idea of our students' proficiencies so we could create need-based groups. Generally, the three small groups we created each worked with the teacher for twenty minutes of the sixty-minute class period. The lessons we planned were designed to respond to what we had identified as their needs. We began to feel a little better about addressing the needs of our students. They responded by showing much greater interest and by making gains in their achievement. But, we were still novices at this game.

Eventually, my school implemented Guided Reading based on the Fountas and Pinnell model (1996, 2001). As we applied this teaching framework to language arts instruction, it became apparent to me that this model was an effective method of teaching for differentiating instruction to meet the needs of my learners. And, with some tweaking, I began to apply it to my math instruction, too. Not only did this method allow me to teach each group at an instructional level that maximized its learning, but by using the approach with both language arts and mathematics, it was easy to establish and teach consistent routines and procedures to students. Soon, some of my colleagues began using what we now call Guided Math.

In my position as an Instructional Coach, I now work with our entire staff as it makes the transition to teaching math using the Guided Math framework. From my communication with teachers across the country, it is obvious that many of them are beginning the process of implementing their own versions of Guided Math. It is my hope that this book will provide some encouragement and guidance to those teachers. There is no one "right" way to use Guided Math. By sharing our ideas, we can help each other implement Guided Math in ways that work best with our teaching styles and in our classrooms.

Laney Sammons

Acknowledgements

The ideas for this book were incubated during my years teaching and then working with teachers as an Instructional Coach at Samuel E. Hubbard Elementary School in Forsyth, Georgia. They were culled from the countless experiences and interactions with some truly inspired teachers and administrators—not to mention children. I thank my principal, Angie Dillon, for the encouragement and support she has given me as the seed for this undertaking was nurtured. My thanks are also extended to Maggie Bowden, who as the Assistant Superintendent of the Monroe County Board of Education in Georgia, led and inspired the Instructional Coaches of the county. My warmest appreciation also goes to friend and colleague Wendy Hamm. She has been a sounding board, a collaborator, and an encourager. The photographs that illustrate this book are hers. To the teachers and other staff members at Hubbard Elementary School, I extend my gratitude. I am privileged to work with such an outstanding staff.

As always, my family sustained me as I worked on this book. Although they no longer live nearby, my daughter Sorrel and son Lanier, along with their families, constantly checked on my progress and offered encouragement. My apologies to my grandchildren, Ash and Griff, who have been somewhat neglected by their Nonny. I promise I will make it up to you.

During the past few months as I worked at school during the day and wrote in the evenings and on weekends, I literally could not have survived without the support of my husband. He assumed my daily chores and obligations, fed me dinner, and listened to my many complaints about technology problems. I thank you for your love and encouragement, Jack. Please know that it is returned.

And, finally, thank you to Emily Smith and Sara Johnson, my editors, for offering me the opportunity to share my thoughts about Guided Math through this book.

Guided Math: A Framework for Mathematics Instruction

Think back to your elementary school days. Picture your math classes. What do you remember? Many of us recall instructions to get out our math books and open to a specified page. The teacher explains the lesson using the chalkboard or overhead projector. One or two students may be called on to solve problems at the board as the rest of the students practice at their desks. Some of us may remember using manipulatives in our early grades, but probably not beyond second grade. Finally, problems from the book are assigned for classwork or homework. These assignments are later turned in to be checked and graded. Periodically, quizzes are given to check on understanding. At the end of the chapter, a test is given. The teacher then moves to the next chapter.

Was this method successful? For many of us, the answer is yes. The teacher-centered approach provided the instruction we needed. We applied this instruction to problems to be completed, and our understanding increased. If it didn't, we comforted ourselves with the knowledge that some people just don't have mathematical minds. We often decided to make the most of our other skills. Many of us simply opted out of math classes as soon as we could. All too often in the past, this was considered good enough. Students either "got it" or they didn't. Their grades indicated how well they "got it."

Unfortunately, too many of us "didn't get it." Mathematical literacy is a serious problem in the United States (U.S. Department of Education 2008). Seventy-eight percent of adults cannot explain how to compute the interest paid on a loan, 71% cannot calculate miles per gallon on a trip, and 58% cannot calculate a 10% tip for a lunch bill (Phillips 2007). According to the U.S. Department of Education's National Mathematics Advisory Panel, "there are persistent disparities in mathematics achievement related to race and income—disparities that are not only devastating for the individuals and families but also project poorly for the nation's future, given the youthfulness and high growth rates of the largest minority populations" (2008).

In spite of the evidence that too many of our students are struggling with mathematics, the traditional, whole-class instructional method continues to be what most students encounter in today's schools. Whereas instruction in reading has changed dramatically over the last twenty years, the teacher-centered, large-group instruction model of teaching is still prominent in mathematics classes across the nation.

Because of the limitations of this method of instruction, students are often presented with the message that there is a particular way in which mathematics must be done—that there is only one right answer and only one right way to find that answer. The emphasis is on learning a set procedure rather than on conceptual understanding. Devlin in his book *The Math Instinct* (2005) states, "The problem many people have with school arithmetic is that they never get to the meaning stage; it remains forever an abstract game of formal symbols." As Hyde (2006) points out, by fourth or fifth grade, children seem to have lost the problem solving skills they had when they began kindergarten. Lack of conceptual understanding handicaps many students as they face more difficult math challenges in the upper grades.

Many students who don't "get it" fall further and further behind in mathematics as teachers struggle to find the time to help them. Teachers are frustrated trying to meet the needs of those students while continuing to challenge students who master the concepts quickly. Some students complain of being bored while others fail miserably in understanding the concepts being taught. It is easy to feel caught in the middle of a tug-of-war game when trying to balance the needs of diverse students.

The frustrations felt by educators are only increased by the demands of accountability enacted by state and federal governments. School systems are struggling to eliminate the gaps in achievement between minority and majority students, special education and regular education students, and students receiving free and reduced lunches and the rest of the student population. It is no longer acceptable to have a portion of our students underachieve in mathematics. Although the National Assessment in Educational Progress (NAEP) indicates that some of these gaps are slowly narrowing (National Center for Education Statistics 2004), teachers are searching for effective means to reach *all* of their students and ways to adapt instructional methods to accommodate all levels of learners. Making this task even more complicated is the fact that students who are slower learners for one concept in mathematics may very well be accelerated learners with other concepts.

States are upping the ante by developing new and more demanding math standards based on the standards developed by the National Council of Teachers of Mathematics (2000). Teachers are discovering that methods they have used successfully in the past are no longer working. The demands of the new curriculum standards require new ways of teaching.

As I grappled with these frustrations in my own classroom, I gradually developed a model that offers all students opportunities to develop their mathematical skills at increasingly challenging levels of difficulty with the ultimate goal of helping them gain the ability to function independently in the world of mathematics. I learned the importance of establishing and maintaining classroom frameworks that are organized to support numeracy, just as teachers have done for literacy for many years. As teachers establish a culture of numeracy in their classrooms, they extend the mathematical experiences of students in classrooms by making connections to real-world experiences.

The instructional components of this model include:

1. A Classroom Environment of Numeracy

2. Morning Math Warm-ups and Calendar Board Activities

3. Whole-Class Instruction

4. Guided Math Instruction with Small Groups of Students

5. Math Workshop

6. Individual Conferences

7. An Ongoing System of Assessment

Together, these components allow teachers to support each student's efforts at varying levels according to their needs.

A Classroom Environment of Numeracy

Environments rich in mathematical opportunities for children are essential if we want our children to develop a thorough understanding of mathematics. When students begin to recognize how numbers and problem solving affect their everyday lives, mathematics becomes more meaningful to them. Because learning is both a social and constructive process, children learn best through active engagement in authentic opportunities to use and extend their number senses.

The creation of a classroom environment supporting numeracy enables students to build on their previously acquired knowledge of numbers. An organized mathematical support system for students requires that we encourage children to use manipulatives, compute, compare, categorize, question, estimate, solve problems, converse, and write about their thinking processes. Ideally, a math-rich classroom environment and engaging activities will help students become increasingly aware of mathematical and problem-solving opportunities throughout their everyday lives, thus putting a "math curse" on students as authors Jon Scieszka and Lane Smith describe facetiously in their children's book of that title (1995).

The creation of a community of learners is inherent within a classroom supporting the learning of mathematics. Students who feel respected and supported are willing to take risks in problem solving and to share their thinking with others. Through mathematical dialogue, students construct the meaning of mathematics, developing enduring understandings of the "big" ideas or concepts as they also develop procedural and computational fluency. To establish a learning community, teachers need to understand their students and the mathematical "landscape of learning" (Fosnot and Dolk 2001) through which they hope to guide them. With careful planning, teachers are able to foster the strong social aspects that are integral for learning, to teach behaviors that promote constructive conversation, to organize the physical aspects of their classrooms for immersing students in an environment of numeracy, and to provide classroom procedures for students that allow student participation in all components of the Guided Math framework. Chapter two focuses on ways to establish numeracy-rich environments within the classroom.

Morning Math Warm-ups

Math warm-ups take place in the morning to set the tone of the day. As students arrive, they have assigned tasks to complete. Simple daily activities are provided in which students answer a question or complete a mathematical task. During calendar board activities, the class discusses and analyzes the results.

Students may be asked to add to a Number of the Day Chart in which the teacher selects and writes a number at the top of a sheet of chart paper. Upon arrival, each student is expected to write the number in a different way. According to grade level, the numbers and alternate ways of expressing the number will vary. For example, 4 might be written as *3 + 1* or *6 – 2* by younger children. Older children might choose to record it as *(5 x 4) – (2 x 8)*. Since the ways of writing the number will vary, close observation of the chart will provide the teacher with valuable information about the number sense of individual students as well as an overall picture of the level of understanding of the entire class.

Calendar board activities usually begin with a glance at the calendar and the date. From there, a teacher briefly reviews previously covered mathematical skills, previews upcoming skills, provides practice in rote counting skills or math facts, encourages mental math skills, and engages students in problem-solving activities. Often, students sit on the floor around the calendar board, but sometimes, students remain at their desks to participate in these oral or written activities. This daily warm-up encourages students to nimbly move cognitively from one area of mathematics to another in a nonthreatening, fast-paced way. The predominately oral nature of these activities promotes conversations about mathematical concepts which foster a deeper, more enduring understanding by students. Chapter three explores instructional ideas for mathematical warm-ups.

Whole-Class Instruction

Many educators today are moving away from the traditional, teacher-directed method of instruction. However, this type of instruction can have a place in today's classroom, providing it isn't the only, or primary, method of instruction.

Whole-class instruction requires the least amount of teacher preparation. In its most common form, the teacher introduces the lesson, teaches it as students listen and are questioned, provides a practice activity for students, and either summarizes the lesson or has students summarize it. Traditionally, students remain in their desks, facing the teacher who is at the front of the classroom. Most of us are familiar with this traditional method of teaching from our own days as students. Whole-class instruction remains an option within the Guided Math framework, but rather than being limited to this traditional lesson format, a variety of instructional structures are available to teachers.

Whole-class instruction is an excellent method for presenting activating strategies or literature connections at the beginning of lessons, as well as for ongoing review of mastered concepts. Using this format, teachers may choose to present mini lessons or model problem-solving strategies, thinking aloud as they do so. Moreover, this component can be used as a time for "math congress" when students come together following mathematical investigations to share their discoveries (Fosnot and Dolk 2001). This time is called Math Huddle in my classroom.

Teaching to the whole class is a very straight-forward instructional method, but requires a remarkable amount of teacher skill to do it well. Although it often appears that discourse during this time is "off the cuff," to be effective, teachers must juggle what they know of their students and the mathematical concepts on their "horizons" to guide the conversation with meaningful questions. Even a skillful teacher may be unable to reach some students because of students' lack of attention, boredom, inability to understand the instruction, or their often incorrect confidence that they already know how to do the activity so they don't need to listen. Chapter four offers suggestions as to how to use this method most effectively and when it should be avoided.

Guided Math Instruction with Small Groups of Students

Guided Math instruction is a method of teaching in which teachers assess their students formally or informally, and then group them according to their proficiencies at a given skill. The groups are homogeneous, yet fluid, as individual students' levels of understanding change. This method of mathematics instruction is analogous to Guided Reading instruction as espoused by Fountas and Pinnell in their books *Guided Reading: Good First Teaching for All Children* (1996) and *Guiding Readers and Writers Grades 3–6* (2001).

Using Guided Math instruction, teachers are able to work with small groups that are determined specifically by students' achievement levels and needs. This allows teachers to closely observe student work, monitor student attention, provide strong support for struggling learners, and provide extra challenges for proficient learners.

Using this small-group instructional model, teachers can vary the amount of time they spend instructing students according to the specific needs of those students. For example, when a teacher is introducing a new concept, one group of students may quickly grasp the skill and be able to move on to independent practice. Another group may need significantly more time working directly with the teacher in a small group. Rather than boring those students who have already mastered the concept with continued whole-class instruction, this model allows those students to move on to independent work quickly, freeing teacher time for more intensive instruction with the struggling students.

Not only can the amount of instructional time differ, but so can the content of the material covered and the amount and level of difficulty of the practice work assigned. Guided Math groups offer teachers an efficient way to provide differentiated instruction to meet the needs of diverse learners. Chapter five examines, in greater depth, how to establish and effectively use small groups for Guided Math.

Math Workshop

So, what are the other students doing as the teacher meets with small groups or conferences one-on-one with students? For small group instruction and conferencing to be effective, it should be uninterrupted. Students who are not engaged directly with the teacher must have meaningful work to do and know how to follow established and practiced procedures for independent individual or group work. These students participate in Math Workshop.

As the school year begins, students are taught how to work independently. The teacher establishes expectations and routines during the first few weeks of school. Students learn how to access materials they may need, follow rules for working with manipulatives, handle any questions they may have, and learn what to do if they complete their assigned work. Periodically throughout the year, the teacher may need to revisit these expectations.

Because each instructional minute of the day is so important, it is essential that meaningful work is provided for each student.

Providing something beyond busy work also helps prevent discipline problems because students who are engaged in challenging work are less likely to disrupt the class. Workshop tasks might be inquiries or investigations, math-center activities, math games, problems of the week, Math Journal writing, or written practice to maintain previously learned skills. In chapter six, these activities are described in more detail with suggestions for establishing procedures and routines.

Individual Conferences

Guided Math offers teachers valuable opportunities to interact with students in small groups and observe communication between students as they work. Sometimes, however, one-on-one work is needed to aid the teacher in assessing student understanding of mathematical skills or concepts, to clarify or correct student misunderstandings and errors, or to extend or refine student understanding.

At any time throughout the day, teachers can conference with individual students. In very much the same way that teachers have used reading and writing conferences, they can meet briefly with students to further those students' understanding of mathematical concepts. These individual conferences provide rich information about how to best work with individual students. Additionally, the conferences help teachers identify specific teaching points for individuals and for the class as a whole.

In chapter seven, individual conferences are covered in greater depth. Additionally, a basic structure for individual conferences is presented and methods for recording anecdotal notes are described.

An Ongoing System of Assessment

How do we know how to group students? How do we determine the needs of the class? How do we determine individual needs?

Ongoing accurate assessment provides teachers with timely information about class and individual student needs. In mathematics instruction, a student's level of proficiency can vary drastically from concept to concept. This makes assessing mathematical knowledge and thinking skills more challenging than assessing reading ability, where periodic running records and comprehension questions provide a strong indication of reading level.

Teaching Guided Math is a more complex process than following a textbook chapter by chapter and assigning the same problems for all students in the class. With instructional time so valuable, it is important not to waste time teaching what the students already know. It is also important to refrain from moving ahead page by page, if the students are struggling. But again, how do teachers determine the needs of their students?

A balanced system of assessment gives teachers a complete picture of each child's understanding, not just a single glimpse from a test. Formative and summative assessments, including observations of students' work, discussions with students, and assessment of their finished products, all give valuable perspectives on their capabilities and needs. In addition, to maximize student learning, students themselves must be involved in assessing their own work based on criteria, rubrics, or exemplars. To truly "leave no child behind," assessment should be more than just giving grades on tests and on report cards. Chapter eight examines an overview of both individual and class assessments that allow teachers to refine and extend their instruction to meet the needs of each student.

In Practice

How does Guided Math look in a real classroom? What would one see? Chapter nine provides an overview of how the components of this approach come together and are applied. Guided Math can be implemented by a single classroom teacher, but collaboration among teachers makes the process easier. Teachers may want to choose among the various components of Guided Math using the Menu of Instruction (Figure 1.1). It is often easier for teachers to begin with a few of the components and gradually add more.

Figure 1.1: Guided Math Menu of Instruction

Guided Math: Menu of Instruction

Daily: Classroom Environment of Numeracy—A classroom should be a community where students are surrounded by mathematics. This includes real-life math tasks, data analysis, math word walls, instruments of measurement, mathematical communication, class-created math charts, graphic organizers, calendars, and evidence of problem solving.

Daily: Calendar Math and Morning Work—This daily appetizer prepares the palate for the "Your Choice" entrées below with calendar activities, problems of the day, data work, incredible equations, review of skills to be maintained, and previews of skills to come.

Your Choice: Whole-Class Instruction—The following are excellent teaching strategies to use when students are working at the same level of achievement: introducing lessons with a mini lesson or an activating strategy, teacher modeling and think-alouds, read-alouds of math-related literature, organizing a Math Huddle, reviewing previously mastered skills, setting the stage for Math Workshop, and using written assessments.

Your Choice: Small-Group Instruction—Students are instructed in small groups with changing composition based on their needs. The individualized preparation for these groups offers tantalizing opportunities to introduce new concepts, practice new skills, work with manipulatives, provide intensive and targeted instruction to struggling learners, introduce activities that will later become part of Math Workshop, conduct informal assessments, and reteach based on student needs.

Your Choice: Math Workshop—Students are provided with independent work to complete individually, in pairs, or in cooperative groups. The work may be follow-up from whole-class or small-group instruction, practice of previously mastered skills, investigations, math games, Math Journals, or interdisciplinary work.

Daily: Conferencing—To enhance learning, teachers confer individually with students, informally assess their understandings, provide opportunities for one-on-one mathematical communications, and determine teaching points for individual students, as well as for the class.

Daily: Assessment—Be sure to include a generous helping of assessment *for* learning to inform instruction, with a dollop of assessment *of* learning to top off each unit.

The very nature of this approach to teaching mathematics allows it to be incorporated flexibly into daily schedules. The constant daily features are the environment of numeracy, calendar board, morning work, conferencing, and assessment. All of these can be spread throughout the day. During the block of time allotted for mathematics instruction, a teacher may choose from whole-group instruction; small-group instruction; Math Workshop; or a combination of them based on the level of support needed by the class for the mathematical content being taught.

Levels of support vary according to the instructional approach chosen by the teacher. Figure 1.2 provides an outline of instructional approaches, teacher activities, and support levels that complement the approaches and activities.

Figure 1.2: Levels of Support for the Guided Math Components

Instructional Approach	Teacher Activity	Level of Support
Whole Group	Activating Strategies Modeling Think-Alouds Direct Instruction Mini Lessons Leading Students in formulating conjectures or Math Congresses Directed Review	Full support for all students by the teacher specifying the approach to problem solving or guiding the conversation; teacher has the major responsibility.
Small Group	Facilitates as students explore new concepts and extends understanding of previously introduced concepts	Moderate level of support and targeted instruction based on student needs; more responsibility is released to students as the teacher provides scaffolding for their efforts.
Math Workshop	Provides tasks for independent, individual, or group work by students	Low level of support; tasks should be those which students can complete without teacher assistance; responsibility is shifted to students.

Since the ultimate goal of mathematics instruction is to teach students to solve problems independently, the flexible nature of these components encourages the gradual release of responsibility approach described by Pearson and Gallagher (1983). In the gradual release of responsibility model, teachers provide students with various levels of scaffolds and gradually help them take responsibility for concepts. The gradual release of responsibility begins with the teacher doing most of the work. The whole-class instruction option provides the maximum teacher support. Teachers may lead students through an activating activity to tap students' background knowledge and stimulate interest. Through modeling and think-alouds, teachers can guide students through their thinking as they demonstrate mathematical concepts and problem-solving strategies. Whole-class instruction is primarily a teacher-centered activity. Students listen, answer questions, and turn and talk with partners when requested. The teacher has minimal opportunity to monitor comprehension or communicate with most of the class.

In the next phase of the gradual release of responsibility model, the students are expected to increase their roles in learning the concepts. When working in small, Guided Math groups, the role of the student increases. The teacher carefully provides instruction appropriate to the needs of the group and provides scaffolding to allow students to move beyond their independent capabilities, increasing student responsibility for learning.

The final stage of the gradual release of responsibility model enables the students to take complete responsibility for their learning. In Math Workshop, students assume full responsibility in tasks planned by the teacher. They work independently, individually, or in small groups and should not only be very familiar with the procedures and expectations of the teacher, but should also be able to carry out the assigned work with no additional teacher guidance. Students move through these components, gradually assuming more responsibility for their conceptual understanding and problem-solving skills. Since learning is not usually a completely linear process, the level of teacher support required by students varies from day to day and lesson to lesson. Guided Math offers teachers an instructional framework that encourages students to gradually assume increasing responsibility as they learn, while at the same time providing scaffolding and support when needed.

Figure 1.3, on the following page, shows how these components can be woven together for instruction during the week. On Monday, the entire mathematics period is taught as a whole group as the class begins with an Activating Strategy. A problem is then presented, which the teacher solves by thinking aloud to explain the thought process to the students. Following the problem-solving activity, the independent work for the week is introduced with a mini lesson.

On Tuesday, the class begins with a read-aloud of mathematics-related literature as the whole class gathers to listen and then discusses the mathematical connections. After the read-aloud, students begin independent work in Math Workshop. The tasks were explained on Monday, so students should be ready to begin with little additional direction. For the first fifteen minutes of the Math Workshop, the teacher circulates around the classroom, conferencing with individual students. For the last thirty minutes, the teacher meets with Guided Math group 1. The lesson is tailored specifically to the needs of these students who have been grouped together because of their similar needs. They may be students who have already mastered what most of the students are currently working on and they can be given more challenging instruction. Or, they may be students who the teacher noticed have a particular problem that can be addressed easily through small group instruction. Sometimes, they are students who need additional scaffolding and support with the concepts on which the class is working.

Wednesday's structure is similar to that of Tuesday. The class begins with a mini lesson, but this time a problem is posed for the class to solve and discuss. Math Workshop begins with the teacher engaged in conferencing initially. The teacher meets with Guided Math group 2 after conferencing, which is another group with different needs.

To meet with two groups on Thursday, the teacher dispenses with the mini lesson. Students begin Math Workshop immediately.

The teacher spends fifteen minutes conferencing, followed by thirty minutes with Guided Math group 3. For the last thirty minutes of the class, the teacher meets again with the first group who had met previously on Tuesday, for additional instruction.

The schedule for Friday is quite different. Students meet for whole-class instruction as they participate in a Math Huddle. During this time, they share and discuss their observations, problem-solving strategies, conjectures, or representations with the class. The ideas shared are recorded in a chart or graphic organizer that is posted in the room for future reference.

Figure 1.3 Sample Guided Math Schedule for a Week

Day	Activity	Guided Math Components
Monday	• activating strategy • problem solving think-aloud by teacher • explanation of independent work for the week (investigation, paper/pencil practice, games)	Whole Class
Tuesday	• mini lesson (read-aloud) • independent math work with teacher conferencing for the first 15 minutes • Guided Math with group 1	Whole Class Workshop Conferencing Small Group
Wednesday	• problem challenge mini lesson • independent math work with teacher conferencing for the first 15 minutes • Guided Math with group 2	Whole Class Workshop Conferencing Small Group
Thursday	• independent math work with teacher conferencing for the first 15 minutes • Guided Math with group 3 • Guided Math with group 1	Workshop Conferencing Small Group
Friday	• Math Huddle (students share their observations, problem solving strategies, conjectures, representations) • create a chart or graphic organizer to post in the classroom for reference	Whole Class

This weekly plan is an example of the kind of flexibility the framework offers teachers. When planning, it is important to take into account the curriculum and the students to determine which of the components work best for each day of instruction.

The U.S. Department of Education's National Mathematics Advisory Panel (2008) suggests that research does not support the contention that mathematics instruction should be completely teacher-centered or student-centered. Instead, it should be "informed by high-quality research, when available, and by the best professional judgment and experience of accomplished classroom teachers." Guided Math is a framework for teachers that allows them to use their professional judgment to structure mathematics instruction to meet the diverse needs of the students in their classes. It moves away from the one-size-fits-all model and empowers teachers to determine the best instructional strategies for each student, for the class, and for the concepts being taught each day.

Review and Reflect

Think of the way you currently teach mathematics.

1. What aspects of it are successful?

2. What aspects of it trouble you? Why?

3. Does your math instruction lead your students to a deep conceptual understanding of the math standards that they are learning? If so, what are you doing that contributes to that? If not, how do you think you would like to change your teaching?

Using Guided Math to Create a Classroom Environment of Numeracy

Anyone entering most elementary school classrooms would have no problem determining that reading and writing are being taught there. With overflowing bookshelves, books on desks, poems of the week, alphabet charts, graphic organizers showing story elements, word walls, journals, writing folders, writing centers, vocabulary charts, sets of leveled books, and cozy places to read, it is quite obvious that serious reading and writing are taking place throughout the day. If only the same were true for mathematics! Certainly some signs of mathematics instruction may be evident—manipulatives, math books, posted student work, and perhaps a calendar board. However, compared to the environment of literacy that we have worked so diligently to create for our students, we often neglect to do the same for numeracy.

Professional writing about teaching literacy abounds and encourages teachers to create classroom environments of literacy for their students (Fountas and Pinnell 1996; Fountas and Pinnell 2001; Miller 2002; Calkins 2000; Collins 2004). Fountas and Pinnell describe a classroom where "Every day, every child in the classroom encounters materials that she can read and that are of interest" (1996). As an underlying theory, they state, "Children learn about written language in an environment that is print rich" (1996). Abundant collections of literature, word walls, read-alouds, shared reading, shared writing, interactive writing, writing centers, poetry charts, reading workshop, writing workshop, use of authentic print, and writing for authentic purposes are characteristics of such an environment. Throughout the day, students are immersed in print and conversations about reading and writing. But, more than just these attributes contribute to the creation of the rich climate of learning envisioned by these authors.

Teachers strive to organize their classrooms by interweaving these elements and making them accessible to all. That's not an easy task. It requires forethought and planning; no two teachers will do this in exactly the same manner. The organizational structures teachers create reflect their own teaching styles. Not only must the physical arrangement of the room be conducive to this kind of literacy instruction, but procedures that will facilitate it must be developed and taught to students as well. When planning, skillful teachers give thoughtful consideration to how to instill a love of reading and writing in their students, as this is essential in building a community of literacy learners. Again, this is no easy task, but it is being done effectively in classrooms every day.

If only the same were true for mathematics! The same techniques described above can be adapted to mathematics instruction and are equally as successful. This framework, Guided Math, rests on the foundational principles set forth in the next section.

Foundational Principles of a Guided Math Classroom

- *All children can learn mathematics.* Although No Child Left Behind brought this principle to the forefront, it is something that teachers *know*. It is our responsibility to see that all students are challenged. The U.S. Department of Education's National Mathematics Advisory Panel (2008) reports students' beliefs about learning are directly related to their performance in mathematics. Studies have shown that when they believe that their efforts to learn make them smarter, they are more persistent in pursuing their mathematics learning. Frequently, parents excuse their children's lack of achievement in mathematics as if it were an inherent ability that one either has or doesn't have. Along with challenging our students, we need to create an environment where students recognize the relationship between effort and learning.

- *A numeracy-rich environment promotes mathematical learning by students.* Borrowing from the research regarding literacy education, where immersion in a literacy-rich environment is considered essential to promote learning, it is important that students are immersed in a world of mathematics (Cambourne 1988). As students see numbers and math-related materials throughout the classroom and participate in real-world, meaningful problem-solving opportunities, they begin to see the connection mathematics has to their own lives. Mathematics is no longer solely problems in a textbook, but it becomes something to ponder.

- *Learning at its best is a social process.* Vygotsky (1978) stressed the importance of children verbally expressing their ideas in the process of reasoning for themselves. They develop language through their experiences and begin to generalize their ideas through oral communication with a teacher or with fellow students. Reflective conversation and dialogue within a classroom setting is a tool which allows students to engage with the ideas of others and to construct hypotheses, strategies, and concepts (Nichols 2006). Learning is enhanced as students are at work with others exploring the same ideas (Van de Walle and Lovin 2006).

- *Learning mathematics is a constructive process.* As Fosnot and Dolk (2001) describe mathematical learning, "children learn to recognize, be intrigued by, and explore patterns, as they begin to overlay and interpret experiences, contexts, and phenomena with mathematical questions, tools (tables and charts), and models (the linear Unifix train vs. the circular necklace). They are constructing an understanding of what it really means to be a mathematician— to organize and interpret their world through a mathematical lens. This is the essence of mathematics."

- *An organized classroom environment supports the learning process.* Efficient organization of materials, use of time, and procedures established for students contribute to the effectiveness of the learning environment.

- *Modeling and think-alouds, combined with ample opportunities for guided and independent problem solving and purposeful conversations, create a learning environment in which students' mathematical understanding grows.* In the classroom, teachers set the stage for learning. As teachers model problem-solving strategies that include multiple representations and approaches, students become aware that there is rarely only one correct way to approach solving problems. This risk-free environment, where mistakes are viewed as opportunities to learn, encourages students to investigate, recognize relationships, and form generalizations from their experiences. Effective teachers orchestrate instructional strategies based on the content being learned, the needs of the class, and the needs of individual students, with the ultimate goal of supporting *all* students as they begin to understand mathematical "big ideas" and grow proficient at organizing and interpreting the world through a mathematical lens (Fosnot and Dolk 2001).

- *Ultimately, children are responsible for their learning.* As Marilyn Burns (2000) puts it, "You cannot talk a child into learning or tell a child to understand." However, that doesn't mean that a teacher is absolved of responsibility. Educators enjoy the responsibility of establishing the motivation and opportunity for students to learn. Cochran (1991) vividly describes a teacher who understood this principle: "And once I had a teacher who understood. He brought with him the beauty of mathematics. He made me create it for myself. He gave me nothing, and it was more than any other teacher has ever dared to give me."

These principles (Figure 2.1) are adapted from the underlying theories upon which Guided Reading is built, as described by Fountas and Pinnell (1996).

Figure 2.1 The Foundational Principles of Guided Math

The Foundational Principles of Guided Math
All students can learn mathematics.
A numeracy-rich environment promotes mathematical learning by students.
Learning at its best is a social process.
Learning mathematics is a constructive process.
An organized classroom environment supports the learning process.
Modeling and think-alouds, combined with ample opportunities for guided and then independent problem solving and purposeful conversations, create a learning environment in which students' mathematical understanding grows.
Ultimately, students are responsible for their learning.

Building a Classroom Learning Community

Although there is not only one correct way to teach, certainly providing a challenging and supportive classroom learning community is a prerequisite (NCTM 2000). In such a classroom, each student understands that he or she can and, indeed, is expected to engage in making meaning of his or her world mathematically (Fosnot and Dolk 2001). In this learning community, students are not only given opportunities to learn the "big" ideas of mathematics; they also participate in a carefully supported climate of inquiry where ideas are generated, expressed, and justified, thus creatively exploring mathematical relationships and constructing meaning.

The teacher is no longer the "keeper, dispenser, and tester of knowledge." Instead, being part of the community, the teacher shares in the process, acting as a "model, facilitator, and, at times, a co-learner" (Nichols 2006). The role of students shifts from the traditional classroom model where they sit at their desks, listening, answering questions, and receiving information, being filled with knowledge bestowed by the teacher, to one in which students are active participants in their learning.

Of great importance in maintaining a sense of community is respect for all classroom members and the feeling that, as students, they are respected. Students need to know that their efforts are valued and supported by others, that risk-taking and mistakes are part of learning, and that they can be successful. They need to see that mathematics is a creative exploration, a search for patterns and relationships based on mathematical ideas. They need to see that, in this exploration, each member of the community plays an active role—that the contribution of differing perspectives often leads to a more complete understanding by all. The understanding of the entire community is really more than that of each member on his or her own. Thus, the importance of the teacher's role in establishing a classroom community can't be overstated.

In a true classroom community, *each* of its members is respected and valued. Students look to teachers for guidance in how to treat others. When a teacher has high expectations for all students, struggling students tend to live up to expectations, and other students' perceptions of them reflect those expectations. In our society, we tend to believe that only some students are capable of learning mathematics (U.S. Department of Education 2008, NCTM 2000). Even parents often excuse poor achievement by saying that they were never good in math when they were in school, as if mathematical ability were an inherited talent you pass down genetically. Therefore, teachers must convince students, parents, and the community, that expectations are high for all students and that effort and achievement in mathematics are linked.

For mathematics education to be truly equitable, skillful teachers realize that high expectations alone will not provide equity for all students, and without equity for all students in the class, the sense of community flounders. In a Guided Math framework, the components offer teachers a myriad of approaches to provide scaffolding and support for all learners based on their needs.

Communication is at the heart of mathematics—to clarify thinking, to express ideas, to share with others, to justify processes, and to explore relationships. The NCTM Communication Standard (2000) specifies that instructional programs from pre-K to Grade 12 should enable students to:

- organize and consolidate their mathematical thinking through communication
- communicate their mathematical thinking coherently and clearly to peers, teachers, and others
- analyze and evaluate the mathematical thinking and strategies of others
- use the language of mathematics to express mathematical ideas precisely

In addition, the other NCTM process standards (Problem Solving, Reasoning and Proof, Connections, and Representation) rely heavily on student communication. Many states are creating or have already created mathematics curriculum standards based on the NCTM standards. As a result, teachers throughout the United States are grappling with how they can best provide process standard-based instruction for their students. Unfortunately, until recently, many of the traditional textbooks offered minimal instructional materials on these standards. The materials, when provided, most often presented these standards in isolation. Clearly, these standards are meant to be taught *with* the content standards rather than as stand-alone instruction. When compartmentalized, students have difficulty visualizing mathematics as a coherent whole (Hyde 2006). It's ironic that mathematicians have for so long recognized the importance of mathematical communication, yet it has traditionally played such a limited role in elementary-school mathematics instruction.

Worthwhile student conversation and dialogue doesn't just occur because the standards demand it or the teacher values it. Highly effective teachers model and instruct how to communicate ideas. They teach students the give-and-take of conversing. Students learn how to engage with others, to construct hypotheses, to reason, and to justify (Nichols 2006). This accountable or purposeful talk is not just chitchat. It has a process and purpose. As such, it is part of the process by which students construct meaning in the world of mathematics.

In the book *Making Sense* (Hiebert et al. 1997), the authors list four characteristics of a productive classroom community for mathematics in which communication plays a major role.

1. Ideas are the "currency" of the classroom. The ideas of all students have value and can contribute to the learning of the community when shared. Carefully considering the ideas of others is a sign of respect.

2. There is often more than one approach to solving a problem. Students have the freedom to explore alternative methods, and then share them with others. Each student, in return, must respect the ideas and approaches of others. This respect for the ideas shared by others allows genuine classroom conversation to occur.

3. Students must understand that it is okay to make mistakes—that errors are opportunities for growth as they are examined and explained. Rather than being something to be covered up, they become opportunities to explore erroneous reasoning, and therefore, can be used constructively.

4. The correctness or reasonableness of a solution depends on the mathematics itself, rather than the popularity or status of the presenter. Students learn that mathematics makes sense. The focus of discourse is reasoning and logic as it relates to mathematics rather than on satisfying a figure of authority. This understanding frees students to actively explore problem-solving strategies rather than passively waiting for teacher's guidance and engenders confidence in sharing their thinking.

These characteristics are nurtured in classrooms when teachers consider carefully, and then implement, classroom procedures that promote them. This can be accomplished through the establishment of ground rules for discourse and through teacher modeling (Van de Walle and Lovin 2006). In *Thinking Mathematically* (Carpenter, Franke, and Levi 2003), the authors suggest establishing class norms where "students explain their thinking, they listen to one another, and alternative strategies for solving a given problem are valued and discussed." To encourage accountability in conversation and move construction of meaning to new levels, Nichols (2006) suggests that students be taught that purposeful talk means that they must say something meaningful, listen with intent, and keep the lines of thinking alive (in other words, stay focused on the topic being discussed).

Specific practice in the art of conversing can help students perfect their skills in discourse. Often, students are unaware when they either dominate the conversation or are not a part of it at all. Daily talks with parents or peers rarely prepare them for the kinds of dialogue that lead to constructing meaning within a community. Students emulate teachers as they model respectful and worthwhile conversational behavior. Teachers can help children become more aware of who is speaking and of the value of taking turns. Students learn the value of being a listener, reflector, and participant in extending and developing the ideas set forth. As students learn to pause and think before speaking, their comments become more focused. Turning and talking with partners allows students opportunities to practice comments that they may want to share with the group. Sharing one-on-one builds confidence that some students need before they open their thoughts to a larger group. Even turn-and-talk behavior must be taught so that students realize that it isn't just each person sharing an idea—that they are also expected to be listeners who engage with each others' ideas (Nichols 2006). Effective teachers know that this kind of conversational behavior does not develop on its own. They recognize, in planning, that teaching it is their responsibility.

As students become more practiced in conversing respectfully with purpose, teachers find that it strengthens the sense of community in a classroom. Not surprisingly, an increased sense of community then improves the discourse (Nichols 2006).

Classroom Arrangement

At the beginning of school every year, teachers typically grapple with how to set up their classrooms. Aesthetically, they want them to be warm and welcoming. They envision their students as they first enter their new school "home." How will they feel? Teachers ponder ways in which they can create an environment that shows their new students how much they are valued.

In addition to the desire to create a welcoming environment, teachers know that the way they set up their rooms can actually affect student learning. As desks are set out, bulletin boards put up, and learning materials are organized and stowed, teachers are concerned with the more subtle messages that students receive about what is valued in learning (NCTM 2000).

Rows of desks facing forward, few available manipulatives, and the absence of student-created and mathematics-related charts send a clear message that this is a teacher-centered classroom. Students are expected to sit by themselves during lessons. There are no tables or areas available for collaborative discussions or activities. Mathematics instruction becomes a static process instead of an active process.

Other classroom arrangements send different messages altogether to the students. In these classrooms, desks are arranged in groups or students sit at tables. There is a large carpeted space with an easel or whiteboard available. Manipulatives are organized and placed in readily accessible places. There is a table with seating for six students where small groups meet with the teacher. On the walls are class-created charts of conjectures they have made or of problem-solving strategies. An interactive calendar board is displayed. Math Word Walls contain mathematical vocabulary words with definitions and representations. Math-related literature is displayed with student work. Students in these classrooms are clearly creatively engaged in the process of constructing mathematical meaning. In these classrooms, there is evidence of a community of learning at work.

As teachers design their classroom arrangements for Guided Math, they are sensitive to the subtle messages they send and to the effects of the physical layout on not only their students, but on the learning process as well. The overall goals in arranging the classroom setting for Guided Math are as follows:

- establish appropriate spaces for each Guided Math component
- create spaces conducive to the social aspects of learning
- facilitate efficient movement within the classroom
- provide ease of access to materials needed by both students and teacher

Teachers who have already established a classroom arranged to teach Guided Reading have a head start on this process. Their classroom arrangements will most likely be conducive to Guided Math.

In the Guided Math framework, teachers consider how the classroom arrangement can promote student independence during math work. Greater student independence is possible when there are clearly designated work areas and students know how to find, and then replace, the materials that they need as they work. As student capacity to work independently increases, the teacher has more time to address the needs of individual students. During the school year, if it is necessary to modify the arrangement, students can be involved in that process, adding to their sense of ownership and understanding of how the classroom environment affects their work (Fountas and Pinnell 2001).

Home Area

Within the Guided Math classroom, students have their home space where their own supplies are kept and where they begin and end their days. This area may be at desks or at tables. If it is at desks, they should be arranged in groupings so that students are able to interact during learning. Student supplies may be stowed in their desks. If at tables, cubbies or crates are provided to contain students' materials. In either situation, students have easy access to any materials needed for mathematical exploration.

Students should begin their day with math-related morning assignments on which they are expected to start working when they enter the classroom. Students should be thoroughly familiar with morning routines. The tasks to be completed are clear and readily available so that the teacher can focus on individual student needs without having to give directions to the students as they arrive.

Large-Group Meeting Area

Ideally, a teacher sets aside a part of the room for large group gatherings or meetings. A carpeted area, if possible, makes a comfortable gathering place for students. Placement of this area adjacent to a calendar board allows it to be used for lessons related to the daily calendar lesson as well as for any whole-class lesson. In this gathering area, there is an easel with chart paper or a whiteboard that may be used by the teacher and students for mini lessons, modeling, think-alouds, read-alouds, creation of student-created anchor charts, steps in problem solving, or the recording of student conjectures. This area is also supplied with markers, pointers, manipulatives and math-related books. If possible, a hundred chart and number line should be clearly visible to students for reference.

Realistically, not all teachers have classrooms large enough to set aside separate space for a meeting area. Small classrooms with large classes often make this impossible. If space is an issue, teachers can plan placement of desks and/or tables in a way that maximizes the inclusiveness of all students during large-group instruction. If the initial room arrangement doesn't work well, it can always be changed at any time during the school year.

Small-Group Area

Classrooms designed for Guided Math include a table, which accommodates up to six students and a teacher. This table is to be used for small-group instruction. Although a table is preferable, some teachers work with small groups seated on a carpeted area on the floor. Whether working with a group at a table or on the floor, the teacher should arrange the space in order to have an unobstructed view of the rest of the class. To maximize the instructional time with small groups, this area needs to be well-equipped with everything that is needed during lessons. There is a small whiteboard, markers, paper, pencils, erasers, work mats, and manipulatives. Since small-group instruction offers ample opportunities for informal assessment, the teacher has a clipboard or other system for anecdotal notes or record keeping. In addition, it is useful to have student records readily available, as this instruction is tailored to the individual student or group of students. Students who join the group for instruction are told what materials, if any, they will need to bring to the group so that this valuable instructional time is not wasted by students returning to their home areas for materials.

This instructional area is clean and organized.

Math Workshop Area

Working independently in Math Workshop, students use space throughout the classroom. Students working individually may work at desks, tables, or find space on the floor. Groups of students working together have the same options. Students are taught basic procedures concerning where they may work during the first few weeks of school. At times, the teacher will specify the work places for students at the beginning of the workshop, while at other times students are permitted to choose their own work spaces. During this independent work time, students know exactly how to access any materials that they may need and how to return those materials when they are finished. The teacher has also shared expectations about movement around the classroom during workshop time. Again, these procedures are carefully considered by the teacher and then taught at the beginning of the year. These procedures may also need to be reviewed with students or revised at times throughout the year. Since the teacher is involved in small-group instruction or conferring with students during workshop time, students who are not with the teacher are aware of the behavioral expectations and are working independently to ensure that the teacher is uninterrupted.

Organization and Storage of Materials

The expression "a place for everything and everything in its place" is especially apt when considering how to organize the many mathematical resources most teachers accumulate over their years of teaching—materials from math workshops; from textbook adoptions; from purchases by the central office, the school, or the grade level; and materials purchased by the teacher. Not only do teachers need to know where their materials are and be able to find them easily, but if students are to be more self-sufficient and independent during mathematics instruction, they also need to be able to access these materials easily. To reiterate one of the Foundational Principles of Guided Math: *an organized classroom environment supports the learning process.*

The first step in organizing mathematics materials is to sort through them and eliminate any that will not be needed. When the materials are culled, they may be sorted by whether they are for teacher-use only or also for student-use.

Resources primarily for teacher-use are stored in areas available to the teacher and organized so that they can be readily found when needed. The organizational schemes vary from teacher to teacher. This seems like common sense, but it takes time and effort to organize materials. This time is valuable for teachers. Making the choice to spend time organizing is often difficult, but in the long run, it makes teaching much easier and more effective during the school year. The process of sorting and organizing materials is best undertaken at the beginning or end of the school year. For teachers who are not sure exactly how to organize their materials, it is helpful to ask other teachers for suggestions. Using the ideas of others makes it much easier to develop a system of one's own.

Those resources that are to be accessible to students need to be just that. When these materials are well-organized and accessible, students can interact with them independently. This frees the teacher to work with small groups or confer with students. It also makes classroom management easier. Fountas and Pinnell (2001) suggest the following ways to organize materials for Guided Reading. They work equally as well for mathematics materials.

Using shelves and tubs keeps instructional materials neat and organized.

- Place each type of material in a separate container that is appropriate in size and shape.

- Label every container, as well as each space in which containers are stored.

- Don't depend on students to arrange materials on shelves. Have a designated and labeled space for everything.

- Eliminate materials that are not essential. An easy test is to determine whether you have used the materials within the last year. If you haven't, get rid of them! Accumulating materials year after year clutters your classroom and interferes with smart management.

Mathematics materials that students will use should be placed near areas where students will work independently and away from the small-group instruction area. In planning, teachers take into account student traffic patterns to prevent traffic jams and the resulting disruptions as students obtain and return materials.

Students also need clearly defined areas for turning in their work, storing Math Journals, or keeping portfolios of their work. Some teachers use trays, bins, or baskets. Prior to introducing the organization structure to students, everything should be well thought out and materials should be clearly labeled.

A Numeracy-Rich Environment

As literacy-rich environments are essential in teaching reading and writing, so are environments rich in numeracy for teaching mathematics. Mathematical learning is both a social and constructive process (Vygotsky 1978, Steele 1999, Van de Walle and Lovin 2006). Students learn best through active engagement in authentic opportunities to use and extend their number sense and develop a deep understanding of mathematical concepts. The creation of classroom environments supporting numeracy enables students to build on their previously acquired knowledge of numbers. Providing an organized mathematical support system for students requires that we encourage students to use manipulatives, compute, compare, categorize, question, estimate, solve problems, talk, and write about their thinking processes. A classroom that clearly demonstrates the importance of sharing the mathematical ideas of students promotes a culture of mathematical discourse (Ennis and Witeck 2007). Ideally, a mathematically rich classroom environment and engaging tasks will help students become increasingly aware of mathematics and its relationship to their everyday lives.

Student Calendars or Agendas

Many classrooms have monthly calendars posted on display boards or bulletin boards where daily calendar lessons are conducted in large-group settings. Throughout the lessons, students participate by responding to questions as a group or when called upon by the teacher.

While these lessons add to the understanding of many students in the class, to fully engage all students, each student maintains an individual calendar or agenda. As kindergarten students begin the year, each morning they take out their calendar folders and simply point to the day of the month and then mark it off or color it. As the year progresses, they begin to record the numeral in the correct box each day. They may color weekend days in a different color from the weekdays to reinforce those concepts. Some kindergarten teachers have their students create tally charts to indicate the number of days they have been in school.

As students progress from grade to grade, the complexity of the tasks increases. Classroom calendar concepts become more challenging. This is reflected in the individual calendars that students keep. Eventually, the calendars become tools where they learn to organize their time and tasks, practicing organizational skills from which they will benefit throughout their lives. The use of either individual calendars or agendas helps students connect the daily classroom calendar activities to their own daily lives in meaningful ways. Because students do not always recognize that they use mathematics in their daily lives, the role of the teacher is crucial in providing activities that increase their awareness (Bamberger and Oberdorf 2007; NCTM 2000).

Manipulatives

It almost goes without saying that classrooms where mathematics is taught should offer students a wide selection of manipulatives with which they can represent concepts and problems they are studying (Ennis and Witeck 2007). The use of manipulatives provides a concrete representation that establishes an image of the knowledge or concepts in students' minds (Marzano, Pickering, and Pollock 2001). In primary classrooms, they are almost universally used. In more and more upper-grade classrooms, this is also becoming the case.

However, it is important that manipulatives be used effectively and not only for teacher-lead demonstrations. Often, teachers who exclusively use manipulatives in this way feel that it is too time consuming to distribute manipulatives to the entire class or feel that supervising the use of manipulatives with whole-class instruction is difficult. It can be the case in whole-group use that students play with the manipulatives, argue with partners, or won't share, so it is easy to see why some teachers shy away from using manipulatives. However, when used appropriately and effectively, manipulatives are one of the most powerful tools in mathematics instruction.

In a Guided Math classroom, flexibility with the teaching formats allows teachers to demonstrate the use of a manipulative in a whole-class setting, if desired. Later, in small-group instruction, manipulatives are easily distributed and their use supervised. After students learn how to use the manipulatives properly, they may work with them independently during Math Workshop. Throughout this instructional sequence, responsibility for using manipulatives is gradually released to students.

As described earlier in this chapter, manipulatives are clearly labeled and stored in areas where students can both access and return them independently. This accessibility allows students to choose from a variety of manipulatives as they investigate and solve problems independently. When students engage in problem solving using more than one method and making use of a variety of manipulatives, the debriefing discussion that follows provides an opportunity for the class to consider multiple methods of solutions and their validity. As a result, students are prompted to begin to generalize and think more abstractly about the concepts being explored.

Problems of the Day and Problems of the Week

In Guided Math classrooms, teachers take advantage of the natural curiosity of students. Teachers use Problems of the Day and Problems of the Week to encourage students to explore, investigate, and hypothesize—all of which appeal to their inquisitiveness. Their active engagement in problem solving provides them with opportunities to develop their mathematical skills and understandings (O'Connell 2007b).

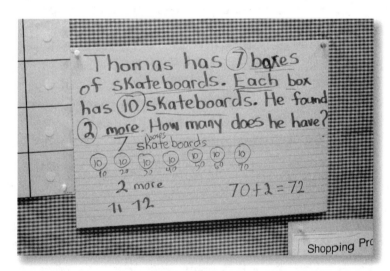

Students solved this Problem of the Day by drawing a diagram.

Students or visitors entering a Guided Math classroom encounter ample evidence of problem solving by the class, by groups of students, and by individual students. Problems of the Day and Problems of the Week are posted and then, when solved, surrounded with various solutions represented in multiple ways to show student problem-solving processes. This highly-visible documentation of mathematics written and drawn by students (in early grades some of it may be done as shared writing—a joint effort of students and teacher) is not intended to simply prove to one and all that much learning has occurred, although it does that, too. The posted work serves as a reminder of successful problem-solving methods and as a jumping off point for further in-depth exploration of problem-solving strategies by students. In later chapters, Problems of the Day and Problems of the Week will be discussed at greater length.

Word Wall and Vocabulary Displays

Mathematics is built on a foundation of a shared, commonly agreed upon vocabulary. The precision of the vocabulary allows mathematical ideas to be expressed and shared. As students enter school, they frequently have the basis for some mathematical concepts. However, the vocabulary for expressing these concepts is often lacking. To engage in mathematical communication, it is imperative that students learn the language of mathematics. Research documents the value of explicit vocabulary instruction in increasing comprehension of new content (Marzano, Pickering, and Pollock 2001). In mathematics, as in other content areas, a focus on vocabulary is essential.

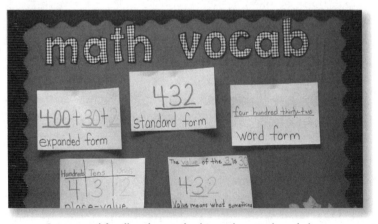

It is essential for all students to develop mathematical vocabulary.

For years, teachers have created word walls. Frequently-used words are posted where they can be seen easily by students. These word walls are created *with* students as new words are identified; they are not already filled with words as the school year begins. Students are expected to use the word wall when they are writing to ensure that their words are spelled correctly. Teachers also use word walls for additional instruction. By playing games, student attention is focused on these words and, more specifically, on letter patterns or other characteristics of the words.

Vocabulary displays are also prominent in many classrooms. These may simply be word banks related to specific topics or units. They may be words that are used frequently in writing, but that may be unfamiliar to the students. Some teachers encourage students to keep vocabulary notebooks in which they define the new words in their own words, use them in sentences, and draw nonlinguistic representations to show their meanings. Vocabulary knowledge is an important foundation as students construct meaning from reading.

Since mathematical vocabulary knowledge is equally important in constructing mathematical meaning, Guided Math teachers borrow many of these techniques to promote the acquisition of mathematical vocabulary. As a new term is introduced, it is added to a Math Word Wall. Most often, the word, its definition, and a representation of the meaning are displayed. Some teachers ask students to create the word cards, thereby increasing students' sense of ownership in the word wall. It is important that the posted words are visible and readable to the students. Word walls are more than passive displays; they are instructional tools. During instruction, teachers frequently refer to the word wall as the class discusses the displayed words. Often, students record new words in their Math Journals along with their definitions and nonlinguistic representations. When students record new words, the teacher checks the Math Journals to be sure words, definitions, and representations are correct. This allows student misconceptions to be identified and corrected before they become established. During mathematics instruction, students frequently consult the Math Word Wall to find just the right word they need to express their mathematical ideas (O'Connell 2007a).

Students are expected to spell the word-wall words correctly and to use them appropriately when they write in their Math Journals or record their mathematical reasoning. Teachers often create games involving the Math Word Walls. For example, a teacher may ask his or her students to write down all of the words that are related to multiplication, and then have them discuss why they chose those words. Or, the teacher may give a definition and have the student find the word with that meaning. The use of these games reinforces the students' knowledge of the meanings of the words and also helps students develop the habit of referring to the word wall when needed. Whenever mathematics is discussed, word walls provide students a readily accessible resource for checking to see that they are using the correct mathematical terminology. As such, it encourages students to assume responsibility for and to monitor their own learning.

Math Journals

The NCTM mathematics process skills emphasize the importance of students' ability to communicate mathematically (2000). Within the classroom, students should have opportunities to hone these skills both orally and in writing. Daily use of Math Journals ensures that children engage in ongoing written mathematical communication, and is evidence of the importance placed on mathematical reasoning in the classroom environment. The use of these journals is appropriate for students throughout elementary school as teachers modify their expectations according to the grade level of their students. Young students create simple drawings to represent their problem solving. Using shared writing (where students work together to compose the sentences while the teacher records them), allows very young students to create class journals of their mathematical thinking. Older students are encouraged to provide nonlinguistic representations of their thinking supported by verbal explanations. O'Connell (2007a) suggests that Math Journals be used by students to:

- brainstorm ideas
- record predictions, observations, and conclusions about mathematical explorations

- list questions
- solve and reflect on mathematical problems
- describe concepts
- justify answers
- explain procedures
- summarize the main points of a mathematics lesson
- make connections between mathematical ideas and other content learning
- reflect on learning in mathematics

The regular recording of mathematical understandings, problem-solving strategies, proofs, and conjectures by students serves several very valuable purposes. As with writing in any content area, the actual process of organizing one's thoughts to express them in writing requires one to reflect and clarify one's thinking. Throughout this process of reflection, uncertainties or even misconceptions may become obvious—ideas that just don't "jive." Planning for writing leads students to monitor and reflect on their own learning, thereby developing their metacognitive abilities. Additionally, by going through the process of thinking and then writing, students have better retention of the concepts.

As teachers read students' journals, they are able to informally assess the understanding of each student. The misconceptions or errors which are discovered aid teachers in planning ways to address them. At times, a misconception may be corrected by a simple one-on-one conference with the student. If a number of students seem to have the same misconception, the teacher may form a small group and address it in that format. Should the misconception be widespread, it may be addressed with the class as a whole or in several small-group sessions. Alternatively, the teacher may plan a hands-on exploration followed by class "debriefing," guiding discussion so that students themselves discover the error.

The kind of notebook used as a Math Journal varies from teacher to teacher. Some prefer to use three-ring binders in which students have dividers to separate their work. Some prefer spiral notebooks. Many use the black and white composition books whose bindings are sewn because they tend to hold up well with daily use. Usually students are required to begin each entry with the date. With daily use, the journal provides a record of learning that students can consult to refresh their memories about concepts or strategies. It may be used for students to complete graphic organizers or record conjectures that have been developed by the class. Some teachers have students write their daily entries starting from the front of the journal. When the class creates conjectures or identifies problem-solving strategies, students record them beginning at the back of the journal. Students can turn back to these pages throughout the year as references.

Math Journals should be readily accessible to students when they are involved in whole-class instruction, small-group instruction, or in Math Workshop. While they may be kept in the students' desks, it often works well to have them stored in a basket or bin where students can access them during mathematics instruction without disturbing the work of others. Wherever they are kept, the system of organization should be clear to all students. They should know that after use, all Math Journals are returned to the storage place. Having the journals stored together in one place allows teachers to quickly check the journals daily without having to gather them from students' home areas.

Graphic Organizers

Graphic organizers are visual diagrams that show the relationships among ideas. According to Fountas and Pinnell (2001), the use of graphic organizers can help students:

- see how ideas are organized or organize their own ideas
- use a concrete representation to understand abstract ideas
- arrange information so it is easier to recall
- understand the hierarchy of ideas (from larger to smaller)
- understand the interrelationship of complex ideas

They can also be used to bridge the connection between a student's prior knowledge, what the student is currently learning, and what the student can apply and transfer to mathematical problem solving in the future (Thompson and Thompson 2005).

Graphic organizers enable students to examine big ideas through the use of diagrams or charts in such a way that relationships and patterns become apparent. Because of the importance of being able to recognize relationships and patterns in mathematical thinking, the use of graphic organizers effectively enhances student understanding of mathematical concepts. The NCTM Standards (2000) state that instructional programs from pre-kindergarten through grade twelve should enable students to "create and use representations to organize, record, and communicate mathematical ideas" and "use representations to model and interpret physical, social, and mathematical phenomena." Graphic organizers assist students by providing a way to represent ideas and communicate their mathematical thinking.

A new graphic organizer is best introduced to students by teacher modeling and think-alouds. The teacher shares his or her thinking while completing the sections of the graphic organizer. Once it is familiar to students, the teacher leads the class or a small group of students in completing the same type of graphic organizer on chart paper, but with different content. Students may also complete individual copies in their Math Journals. Now that students are comfortable working with these graphic organizers, they can be asked to complete ones with the same format independently or as a group project. Both chart-size graphic organizers and smaller, individual graphic organizers are often displayed to remind students of the format of the organizers and how they are used, as well as to provide mathematical content students can refer to whenever necessary.

Many of the graphic organizers used in language arts instruction are easily adapted for use with mathematics. A modified Frayer diagram (Figure 2.2) may be used to promote vocabulary knowledge. Typically, in a Frayer diagram, the vocabulary word goes in the center. At the top-left corner is the definition of the word, at the top-right corner are characteristics of the word, at the bottom-left corner are examples of the word, and at the bottom right are non-examples. In the modified version, students draw a nonlinguistic representation in the upper right-hand corner.

Figure 2.2 Modified Frayer Diagram

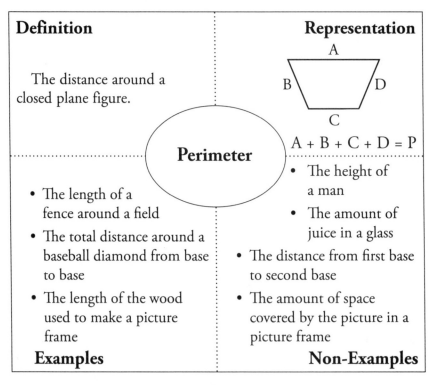

Definition	Representation
The distance around a closed plane figure.	(trapezoid labeled A top, B left, D right, C bottom) $A + B + C + D = P$
Perimeter	
Examples	Non-Examples
• The length of a fence around a field • The total distance around a baseball diamond from base to base • The length of the wood used to make a picture frame	• The height of a man • The amount of juice in a glass • The distance from first base to second base • The amount of space covered by the picture in a picture frame

A graphic organizer for analogies may be used to highlight relationships between mathematical vocabulary words. For example, *sum* is to *addition* as *product* is to *multiplication*. Compare-and-contrast graphic organizers, such as Venn diagrams, may help students analyze the relationship between addition and multiplication by listing ways in which the operations are similar and ways in which they differ. Focusing on these relationships elevates student understanding beyond simple computational proficiency. Similarly, a diagram illustrating steps in a mathematical process serves as a reinforcement of understanding, and later as a reference when posted or recorded in a math journal. It is important that students see various graphic organizers in use and also be given the choice of which to use in a given situation. Unless they have this responsibility, it's difficult for a teacher to determine whether the students really understand the meaning of these organizing structures or if they are only copying what they have seen modeled (Ennis and Witeck 2007).

Class-Made Charts

Classrooms should reflect the learning that occurs within them. In effective reading and writing instruction, classroom charts are developed to brainstorm ideas, to record strategies, to create checklists, to organize or categorize information, to record class stories, and in general, to document what has been going on during language arts instruction. The value of these charts is in the thinking and conversations that led to their creation and also in their use as references when posted in the classroom. It is not uncommon for students to look to where a chart had been hung in order to trigger their memories of the content of the chart long after the chart has been taken down.

In mathematics, class-generated charts can serve the same purposes. Mathematical charts may document problem-solving strategies, provide organizational formats for information, present data collected in ways that make it easy to interpret, display lists of conjectures students have formulated based on their mathematical observations, record steps in a computational process, show the methods used to solve a particular problem, provide illustrations of concepts, or in other ways, reflect classroom discourses. Whether these charts are a result of teacher modeling, shared writing, or interactive writing where the students share the pen with teacher guidance, they often serve as models of mathematical communication.

Miller (2002) records student talk in a notebook and creates large charts to help make the thinking permanent. She writes a note of explanation at the top and then adds snippets of conversations, comments, and statements that reflect the communication during the lesson. According to Miller, these anchor charts "make our thinking permanent and visible, and so allow us to make connections from one strategy to another, clarify a point, build on earlier learning, and simply remember a specific lesson" (2002). Students working independently are able to refer to these charts to find examples of the way mathematical ideas are expressed (Hoyt 2002).

One of the most important aspects of these charts, however, is that they be created in the classroom with student participation rather than being commercial charts or ones made by the teacher without student input. These charts truly reflect and enhance the learning that happens in the classroom.

Tools for Measuring

Often, instruments for measuring appear only when a unit involving that kind of measurement is being taught and are used only during mathematics, or maybe science. Children see these tools as pertaining solely to a specific unit of study rather than as objects used in everyday life. When tools for measuring are displayed in the classroom and used on a regular basis for daily routines and problem solving, students begin to value their utility and understand their importance.

Thermometers in the classroom may be used regularly to check the temperature indoors if it seems a little too warm or too cool, rather than being used solely during a weather unit to check outdoor temperatures. Measuring cups and spoons used during cooking activities or used to measure food for classroom pets help students connect them to daily use in their homes. Meter sticks or rulers are useful when students are involved in creating classroom displays or projects. Student investigations and problems created by teachers that include measurement, encourage the regular use of these tools, and help students develop proficiency in using them.

Measurement can assist students in visualizing what they read. If, for example, a character is described as being four feet (1.2 meters) tall, few students actually have a sense of how tall that is unless they get a yardstick and measure it for themselves. If they read that the winning pumpkin weighed 100 pounds (45 kg) at the fair, most students have no concept of how heavy that is unless they are able to experiment by weighing items. Visualization is a skill that is especially important in reading nonfiction expository texts, which often rely on the concepts of size, weight, length, distance, and time (Harvey and Goudvis 2000). Teachers who encourage students to pay close attention to descriptions and then use tools, when necessary, help their students improve their abilities to visualize. Visualization helps them engage more deeply with the text (Keene and Zimmermann 1997). As a result, these students become better readers. In turn, the visualization strategies practiced in reading enhance mathematical problem-solving capabilities by improving students' abilities to create mental images of problems they are asked to solve (Hyde 2006).

Involvement in science experiments is an obvious time for students to use measuring tools in a meaningful way and to help them experience firsthand the relationship between the two disciplines. Measurement even plays a significant role in helping students understand social studies. How can a student have a true sense of what the conditions must have been like on the *Amistad* unless he or she has a sense of the dimensions of the tiny ship into which so many slaves were packed for an ocean voyage lasting for weeks? When students participate in many "virtual" experiences through the Internet and videos, a sense of scale is frequently missing. What better time to encourage the use of measurement! In this way, students can practice measurement skills, develop a sense of scale, and more fully understand the content of other disciplines.

Math-Related Children's Literature

Literature related to mathematical concepts has enormous power in classrooms. The lure of quality narratives or nonfiction spurs students to make vivid connections to their own lives and to the world around them. Students who are immersed in literary content of many genres are highly engaged by the text and illustrations as mathematical concepts are identified and explored. According to O'Connell (2007a), using children's literature "provides a fun and engaging way to hear about and talk about math ideas. Through story events, students can see math in action." Whitin and Whitin (2000) describe three ways in which literature may be used in mathematical instruction:

- as a vehicle to examine mathematical patterns
- to promote an understanding of large numbers
- to explore the meaning of mathematical vocabulary

An initial read-aloud by the teacher supports the understanding of the text by all students, even those students who may be unable to read it independently. Reading comprehension strategies, such as making connections, asking questions, visualizing, inferring and predicting, determining importance, and synthesizing employed prior to, during, and following the reading, support students in building a true understanding of the text (Keene and Zimmermann 1997; Harvey and Goudvis 2000). Use of these strategies during read-alouds models ways in which they are useful in mathematical problem-solving situations. The strategies help students as they endeavor to clearly understand the circumstances in those problems. Once students clearly understand the story or information from the text, teachers can guide the class to focus on the mathematical relevance of the material using carefully crafted questions. Follow-up instruction challenges students to find the mathematics in the story (O'Connell 2007a) and provides opportunities for students to investigate issues or solve problems from or related to the text. Students are better able to understand mathematical concepts and to communicate their understanding when filtered through the lens of a story. Even after instruction based on a particular book has ended, it should remain on display and be available for students to reread and refer to throughout the day.

By focusing on the relationship between mathematics and literature, students begin to spot mathematical connections in other stories and books. Experienced teachers are quick to encourage students to explore these connections as they emerge. Frequently, the questions or interests of one student are contagious and motivate the entire class to investigate the questions raised.

Math Books by Student Authors

As students practice their mathematical communication skills and experience math-related literature, a logical extension is to encourage them to create their own math-related books. Throughout the year, teachers feel the time crunch and realize that there are not enough minutes in the day to teach everything required—writing about *math* during Writer's Workshop or *writing* during math class optimizes the use of instructional time.

These student-created books may be simple mini books of mathematical vocabulary or explanations of mathematical concepts (O'Connell 2007a). Brightly colored paper foldables such as accordion books, flipbooks, or tri-fold books can be constructed by students. The process of creating these 3-D, interactive graphic organizers is highly motivating and engages students in organizing and communicating mathematical ideas. For examples of the many foldables students can create, consult Dinah Zike's *Big Book of Math* (2003).

Conversely, students may choose to complete complex narrative or informational texts. Students often enjoy creating math-related texts modeled on texts that have been read to them during read-alouds. When their work is based on mentor texts, students are challenged as they emulate the ideas and writing styles found in these familiar books. Their take-offs on these trade books often offer an authentic perspective to which other students relate.

Before expecting students to create books independently, the teacher may lead the class in composing a class book, possibly based on the format of a favorite story they have read and discussed. In primary grades, the process may begin with shared writing. Students can create the sentences and content while the teacher acts as a scribe. Later, it may involve interactive writing in which students work together, guided by the teacher. But at times, with teacher guidance, students actually write selected words from the text. Older students may work together to come up with the overall plan for the book, but the responsibility for writing the pages is assigned to different students. In all of these cases, students are the illustrators.

Since the illustrations themselves are most often representations of mathematical concepts, this activity reinforces student understanding of mathematical concepts.

Although they are writing math books, students are still expected to follow the writing process. They plan their writing, write drafts, revise, edit, and finally publish their work. Because they have been exposed to math-related writing of a variety of genres, students have many models on which to base their own writing. In conferencing with students about this writing, teachers are able to address both writing and mathematical teaching points.

Student published books should be prominently displayed in the classroom or media center as a motivation to others to become authors. In addition, teachers may arrange for student authors to read their books in other classrooms. Many schools have classes who are "reading buddies." Reading buddies may write books, which focus on mathematics, for each other to read. Older students enjoy creating books to share with younger partners, especially when they feel they are helping them learn. Teachers working together may develop additional recognition for young authors as they emulate the math-related writing they have read. Knowing that other students will be reading their books also motivates students to create quality products.

Math Connections to Other Curricular Areas

Implicit throughout this chapter is the notion that students learn mathematics best when they see it as an integral part of their world, both in school and at home. Without a doubt, mathematics plays an enormous role in our lives. In fact, NCTM describes the development of mathematical ideas and the use of mathematics in other disciplines as being intertwined (NCTM 2000). As the interrelatedness of mathematical ideas to other content areas becomes obvious to students, they also become aware of the utility of mathematics.

So, why is it that mathematics is often isolated as a subject in our classrooms? When we help our students become aware of the role mathematics plays throughout the curriculum, they develop a much more expansive and complex understanding. This occurs when teachers explicitly demonstrate the links between mathematics and the other disciplines they teach. This chapter has addressed the reading and writing connections; it also touched on the mathematics and science and mathematics and social studies connections.

As a teacher, I had a large map in the front of my classroom. Any time places were mentioned, in whatever subject areas we were working, I pulled the map down and we located that place. It became second nature to me and to my students. They came to understand the importance of place. If, for some reason, I neglected to refer to the map, my students reminded me. The same should be true for mathematical connections. When teachers develop a "radar" awareness of mathematical connections as they teach, they will find that the connections abound. Moreover, students will develop the same keen awareness. As students' awareness increases, so does their interest. Soon, they begin to notice these connections in their world beyond the classroom. As their interest increases, so does their curiosity about the mathematical connections they discover. To them, mathematics becomes more than algorithms, more than a set of procedures to follow, more than a set of memorized facts—it becomes a discipline that makes sense and is a real part of their world.

...act Amt:	Nearest 10	Nearest 100	Nearest 1,000
Washington Marriott 3 nights $4,514	$4,510	$4,500	5,000
Dinner in Washington and shuttle ride back from ATL Airport $779	$780	$800	$1,000
Savannah Westin conference Registr. $2,705	2,710	$2,700	$3,000
Savannah Westin			

In this cross-curricular activity, students learn that rounding is important when planning a budget for a trip.

Chapter Snapshot

An abundance of evidence of mathematical links in the classroom encourages students to see mathematics as an integral part of their lives. As they observe the seamless connection of mathematics to the everyday world, they develop an expanding curiosity about it. This curiosity spurs their motivation to investigate mathematical relationships more deeply. Teachers play a major role in creating this environment. As teachers stimulate, focus, and direct learning, students not only learn the necessary procedures to solve mathematical problems, but also begin to understand why and how those procedures work, allowing them at first to glimpse, and then eventually grasp, the complex patterns and relationships in the world of mathematics.

Review and Reflect

1. Look back at the Foundational Principles of Guided Math (page 37). Which do you think are the two most important of these principles? Why? How does your classroom reflect those principles?

2. Do you think your students feel that they are members of a mathematical learning community? If so, how did you establish that feeling of community? If not, what can you do to create it?

3. Look at your classroom through the eyes of a new student. Walking into your class, what would he or she see that would indicate the importance of mathematics?

Using Math Warm-ups in Guided Math

Each and every school day begins with students stepping over the thresholds of our classrooms wondering what the day will bring. Some of these students enter with a sense of excitement and wonder. A few look to the teacher, eager to begin. Others straggle in slowly dragging their book bags, lagging as they unpack their belongings. Several students boisterously entertain other students with tales of their morning adventures. Perhaps one student wears an expression that clearly indicates the difficult morning he or she has experienced. As teachers, we are responsible for these young people. No matter how they feel as they arrive, they are here to learn, and we are here to teach them. As we plan our lessons, we ask ourselves how we can stimulate their curiosity, motivate them, guide them, and challenge them—all of them, without exception.

The morning routine we establish sets the tone for the day. Students need to know exactly what they are expected to do upon entering the classroom. It is important to create and teach procedures for unpacking book bags, turning in homework, paying lunch money, using the restroom, and, most importantly, beginning to work.

In a classroom focused on mathematics, this valuable time of the day also serves as a math "warm-up." Having just arrived, students need time to shift gears from family conversations, rides on the school bus, and chats with friends, to readying themselves for school. So, as soon as the students complete their morning "housekeeping" chores, they should be engaged in mini math activities that touch a range of mathematical concepts. Some activities require students to review concepts already covered and mastered. Some relate to mathematical concepts being explored currently. Some give students a preview or taste of concepts to be introduced or extended. Although these activities are short in duration, they are carefully planned, based on the standards being taught and the needs of the students. The teacher is well aware of these individual needs because of ongoing formative formal and informal assessments.

Participating in a variety of *brief* mathematical activities during the first 20–30 minutes of the day leads students to make subtle mental shifts into the world of mathematical awareness and learning. The activities may vary from day to day, but whatever the activities, students should clearly know the expectations regarding behavior and academic work. The morning math warm-up includes one or two tasks that can be completed quickly by each student and which later can be discussed by the class. These can include maintaining a math current-events board, carrying out real-life math-related classroom responsibilities, and completing calendar instruction, which often includes a daily problem to be solved.

The *daily repetition* of a variety of similar tasks and the accompanying class discussions help students to begin to see patterns and make generalizations from these examples. Students develop personal understandings of mathematics concepts when they connect their experiences and background knowledge to the real-life examples and explanations provided by their teachers. Additionally, students are able to "conditionalize" what they know. For example, rather than rote memorization of an algorithm, students understand the conditions under which it can be used appropriately as a result of their conceptual understandings (Hyde 2006).

Math Stretches to Begin the Day

Athletes understand the wisdom in warming-up prior to long, strenuous workouts. They know that by beginning with stretching and a slightly slower pace for a short time, they can maximize their performances over the long haul. In some ways, the same is true for our students. As we present them with one or two mathematical stretching activities, they begin to draw on their prior knowledge and bring this knowledge into their working memories where it can be easily accessed for extending their understanding of mathematics. Students come to look forward to these "stretches," often wondering what they will be asked to do as they arrive at school. The nonthreatening nature of the tasks allows all students to participate independently and with confidence.

Because of the inclusion of all students in the activity, they are eager to be a part of the follow-up class conversation. During this discussion, the students are the primary contributors. The teacher facilitates the learning dialogue to establish a respectful ambience, encourage student participation, model the appropriate use of mathematical vocabulary, guide students to recognize patterns and relationships that might be observed in the event, and focus attention on the relationship of the task to mathematical "big ideas." The brief duration of the discussion makes the role of the teacher critical. As teachers gain experience, they become adept at recognizing student comments and observations that can lead the class to construct meaning from these mini math activities. They also gain experience in using highly focused questions that prompt students to dig deeper in their thinking.

Math stretching activities will vary according to grade level, mathematical standards being addressed, and students' needs. As teachers plan, they must take into consideration these three concerns. In addition, a Math Stretch must be relatively simple so that it doesn't take much time, and it must be able to be completed independently by students with a minimal amount of direction by the teacher. The following Math Stretches are examples and can be adapted to work in any classroom.

Data Collection and Analysis Math Stretch

The National Council of Teachers of Mathematics (2000) placed increased emphasis on data analysis in their mathematics standards. The standard states that students in elementary school should be able to:

- formulate questions that can be addressed with data and collect, organize, and display relevant data to answer them
- select and use appropriate statistical methods to analyze data
- develop and evaluate inferences and predictions that are based on data

This data-collection activity can also be used as a way of taking attendance.

Students have enormous curiosity about the world around them, especially their immediate world. Teachers can take advantage of this characteristic by posing questions for students to respond to as they arrive at the classroom, thus providing opportunities for data collection and analysis. For younger students, the questions are quite simple. In a kindergarten class, it may be, "How did you get to school today?" For older students, the questions presented are more complex and reflect the interests of the students. They may be asked to choose a favorite sport, entertainer, author, or movie from several choices. Students are delighted to be asked questions that they feel confident answering and are eager to take part in the data collection.

 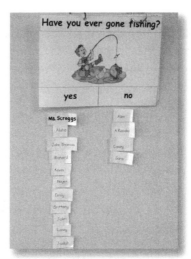

Using Clearly-formulated question enables this type of Math Stretch to be implemented in a short amount of time.

Initially, the teacher creates these questions. Since this stretch is designed to be brief, the answer choices should be limited to no more than four. As students become more aware of the data-collection process, the teacher can request student input in generating questions for this morning Math Stretch. Students who are invested in the process of gathering data because they helped choose the question and are interested in the topic find meaning in their subsequent analysis of collecting data rather than seeing it as a mindless task of generating a series of numbers solely to discern patterns and tendencies (Ennis and Witeck 2007).

For this morning Math Stretch, students are provided with a method for responding and a class graph is created to represent their responses. Depending on the age of the students, their previous experiences, and the subject of the data being gathered, the graph may be a "real" graph, a pictograph, or a symbolic graph.

A "real" graph uses the actual objects being graphed. For example, if students were asked which snack they prefer, cheese crackers or peanut butter crackers, the teacher may provide a basket of each. To respond, each student would choose the package of his or her choice and place it on a grid provided by the teacher, creating a visual representation of the preferences. Or, students might be asked to indicate whether they are wearing shoes with laces or shoes without laces by placing one of their shoes on the grid. Obviously, the use of "real" graphs is limited. However, it does provide a vivid display of data that especially attracts the interest of younger students.

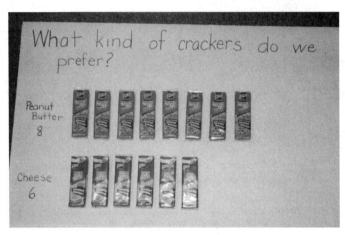

This type of pictograph enables students to actually see the information that is used as data.

A pictograph uses drawings of the objects being graphed. These might be computer-generated pictures provided by the teacher, die-cut shapes, or pictures drawn by the students themselves. With the advent of interactive whiteboards in the classroom, teachers are able to design a graphing task displayed on the board where students can drag pictorial images to the graph. Since time is of the essence during morning warm-ups, teachers usually provide the pictorial representations for the students rather than having students create their own. Student-created pictures may be used in data-representation tasks during other components of Guided Math.

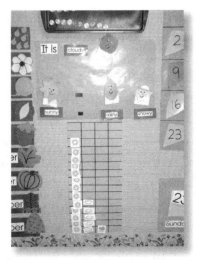

This pictograph displays the weather.

A symbolic graph uses linking cubes, clothes pins, sticky notes, tallies, squares, circles, or other marks to represent the objects being graphed. This is often the graph of choice for these Math Stretches. These graphs can be composed of a variety of materials and be quickly completed by an entire class.

It is important to collect data that is meaningful to the students' lives.

Before a particular method of graphic representation is used for a morning Math Stretch, it should have been previously introduced to the class. Students should be familiar with the type of graph being used and able to work independently in constructing it. To ensure that data collection and representation proceed smoothly, teachers should consider the following steps.

1. Carefully consider the question being posed to be sure it is clearly stated and to anticipate any confusion students may have.

2. Prepare the graphing format in advance and decide what groups of data will be represented and how.

3. Have all materials available and clearly labeled for students as they enter the classroom.

As students contribute their responses, they become curious about their classmates' answers and are drawn to the graphic representation the class is creating. Immediately, students will want to analyze it. They excitedly watch to see their classmates' responses, and they often initially see this as a game having winners and losers. Later, a well-focused discussion about the data gathered corrects this misconception.

When the data display is complete, the teacher brings students together for an analysis of the data. It is this aspect of the lesson that is of most value in helping students understand data collection. Teachers must keep in mind the observations and inferences about the data that they want students to make and skillfully use questioning to scaffold student efforts to interpret the data.

Throughout the year, the content and structure of these discussions will vary depending on the experience and needs of the class. Consistent with the instructional strategy by which teachers gradually release responsibility to the students, these discussions move from teacher think-alouds where the teacher support is strong, to independent student analysis, both oral and written, where students shoulder the responsibility for analysis. (See Figure 3.1 on page 77.)

Initially, teachers must think aloud to share their interpretations of the data collected. They discuss why the data being gathered is important and what they hope to learn from it. In addition, their comments evaluate the kind of graphic display being used and how effective it is in presenting the data clearly in a way that makes analysis easy. The teachers describe what they observe and what they can infer from these observations. Throughout the think aloud, they model the use of relevant mathematical vocabulary. As they share their thoughts, they often record the most significant points on chart paper. As students assume more responsibility during these Math Stretches, they can turn to the chart as a reference.

Once students begin to see what data analysis looks like, the teacher's role gradually changes. Rather than using a think-aloud, they begin to guide the student discussion of the data using carefully crafted questions. Students are encouraged to not only share the facts from the data collected, but also to begin thinking about the inferences they can make. At times, the teacher may rephrase a student observation or comment to use the appropriate mathematical vocabulary or state a concept more clearly. The teacher questioning leads students to consider the meaning of the data and the choice of graph or chart used. Important observations and inferences about the data may be recorded on chart paper by the teacher for future reference. This brief discussion provides the teacher insight into student understanding or misunderstandings and helps guide future instruction (O'Connell 2007).

As students become more proficient at data analysis, teachers step back to become facilitators of the discussion. They may provide some broad, open-ended questions to start the discussion or move it along if it stalls. They ensure that the talk remains focused and that all students feel comfortable participating.

The eventual goal of each student recording thoughts in his or her Math Journal directly reflects the NCTM Communication Standard (2000). It states that all students should be able to organize and consolidate their mathematical thinking through communication, communicate their mathematical thinking to others, analyze and evaluate the mathematical thinking and strategies of others, and use the language of mathematics to express mathematical ideas precisely. The discourse ensuing from the data analysis promotes these standards as students share their reflections and listen to others.

Eventually, when students have demonstrated their understanding of the process, they are asked to record their own analysis in their Math Journals prior to the class discussion. Writing ideas in their journals prior to the discussion helps them to formalize them, set them down on paper so they can actually see and consider them, and, as a consequence, revise them if needed (O'Connell 2007). This in no way eliminates the need for a discussion, however. Students bring their journals to the meeting area to consult as they share what they learned from the data. The actual conversation about the data may prompt some students to change their ideas or expand them. They are encouraged to make these changes in their Math Journals. Students become the primary participants in this math talk. The teacher by no means abandons the discussion. It is essential that the teacher be present to help correct misconceptions and to continue the ongoing informal assessment of individuals and the class as a whole.

Figure 3.1 Types of Discussions

Discussion Type	Teacher Role	Level of Support
Think-Aloud	• Discusses the reason for choosing the particular graphic representation • Shares observations and inferences she or he has made • Models the use of relevant mathematical vocabulary • Records analysis on chart paper for future reference	Highest level of teacher support
Guided	• Uses carefully crafted questions to guide discussion of observations and inferences from the data • Occasionally rephrases student comments to model relevant mathematical vocabulary and concepts • Helps students consider the appropriateness of the graphic representation • Records analysis on chart paper for future reference	Moderate to high level of teacher support
Facilitated	• Poses open-ended questions to stimulate discussion by students • Ensures that discussion stays focused on observations, inferences, and choices of graphing representation • Analysis may be recorded on chart paper by student or teacher or in student Math Journals	Low to moderate level of teacher support
Independent	• Records observations, inferences, and choice of graphing representation by students in Math Journals before discussion • Discussion of journal reflections primarily by students with teacher support, if necessary, to focus discussion or correct misconceptions	Low level of teacher support

In a variation of this activity for older students, a data-collection question may be posed, but students are asked to create their own individual graphs based on this data. The discussion generated would include not only an analysis of the data, but also a discussion of the types of graphs students chose to make (bar, line, circle, etc.), why they chose them, and whether they effectively displayed the data from the question.

Number of the Day Math Stretch

Promoting number sense is a foundation of mathematics instruction. The NCTM standards (2000) state that students should be able to "understand numbers, ways of representing numbers, relationships among numbers, and number systems." More specifically, students in pre-kindergarten through grade two should "develop a sense of whole numbers and represent and use them in flexible ways including relating, composing, and decomposing numbers," while in grades three through five they should "understand the place-value structure of the base-ten number system and be able to represent and compare whole numbers and decimals" and "recognize equivalent representations for the same number and generate them by decomposing and composing numbers." A morning Math Stretch using a Number of the Day Chart addresses these standards and is flexible enough to be adapted for use in classrooms at any grade level.

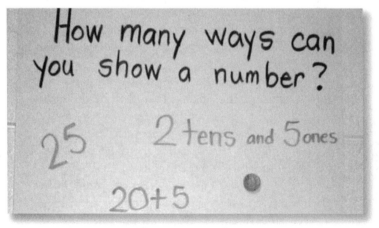

All students should be able to represent numbers in a variety of ways.

When a Number of the Day Chart is used, a teacher writes a numeral on a sheet of chart paper, a whiteboard, or an interactive whiteboard. As students arrive, they are expected to record different representations of that number. In kindergarten, the numeral on the chart might be 5. On the chart, one student might draw five circles, while another student might draw five dots. A student who is beginning to understand how to compose numbers may write *3 + 2*. Another student may write *five*. In a third-grade classroom, a chart might have the numeral *48*. Alternative representations might include *4 x 12*, *40 + 8*, *4 tens and 8 ones*, *10 + 10 + 10 + 10 + 8*, *4 dozen*, or *24 + 24*. A fifth-grade teacher may post the fraction *5/20*. Student responses may be *1/4*, *.25*, *4/20 + 1/20*, *5 x 1/20*, and *1 ÷ 4*.

Each student's representation of the number of the day reflects his or her understanding and as such provides a quick method of informal assessment for the teacher. As the chart evolves, students become curious about the recordings of others. Impromptu conversations between students spur interest as they share their thinking with their peers. Students learn from each other.

When every student has participated in this Math Stretch, the class gathers to examine the responses and determine their validity. Students are asked to explain their reasoning behind their representations of the given number. Manipulatives are readily available for use by students to model their reasoning. The use of manipulatives in the discussion serves as a scaffold for those students who are just approaching the understanding of a particular representation. The combination of explanation by a peer, hands-on modeling, and skillful teacher questioning often leads to "Ah-ha!" moments for students who would not be able to make this conceptual leap independently. By focusing on multiple representations of the same number, students begin to recognize patterns and relationships from which they can draw generalizations or conjectures. Students engaged in these conversations are steeped in mathematical ways of thinking, examining "big ideas" and deciding how best to express them (Carpenter, Franke, and Levi 2003). As the teacher listens to these discussions, knowledge about students' mathematical understanding expands, and this enables teachers to more accurately plan future instruction that meets students' needs.

What's Next? Math Stretch

Since recognizing patterns and relationships is an integral aspect of understanding mathematics (NCTM 2000), a What's Next? chart can be a valuable learning experience for students as they warm-up mathematically. The teacher creates a What's Next? chart by beginning a pattern on chart paper, followed by a blank space for each student in the class. As students arrive in the morning, they study the pattern to decide what comes next. Students take turns filling in the next step in the pattern in the first blank space and put their initials by it. If a student thinks the answer of the previous student was incorrect, he or she can go to the student to discuss it, but may not change it. The only one who may change the answer is the student who recorded it. This may, of course, become a group discussion as other students join in.

The responsibility for correctly extending the pattern rests squarely on the shoulders of the students. In their desire to correctly continue the pattern, they are motivated to work together in arriving at a solution with which they can all be satisfied. Since students must be well-versed in knowing how to respectfully discuss ideas on which they may not agree, this Math Stretch should not be undertaken until the class has established a sense of community where all members and their ideas are valued. Ultimately, in a group discussion facilitated by the teacher, the class comes to a consensus on not only what is next, but also on why it comes next.

The value of this Math Stretch lies as much in the conversation that flourishes, as students exchange ideas, as in the exploration of patterns. Students working on their own tend to work with blinders on, locked into thinking about a problem in only one way. Discussing the problem with others leads to multiple approaches. Peer interaction is especially effective in promoting reflection because the comments and differences in thinking of classmates are most likely within a range that spurs genuine intellectual conflict (Hiebert et al. 1997).

Although the teacher may be tempted to correct mistaken attempts at continuing the pattern, to do so would prevent the genuine reflective conversations that are generated by the students themselves in their search for common ground. Mistakes are a natural part of the learning process and should play an important role as students struggle to comb out meaning from their mathematical experiences. The internal conflict created by discussion among students concerning misconceptions and errors leads them to reevaluate their thinking and clarify their ideas. They become more willing to tackle challenging problems as they discover that errors are not treated as failures, but instead are seen as valued attempts at problem solving and as learning opportunities.

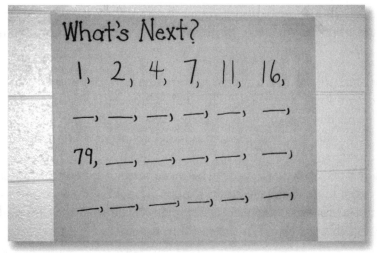

Understanding number patterns is an essential concept for all students because it is the foundation for algebra.

How Did My Family Use Math Last Night? Math Stretch

Students in elementary school view mathematics in many ways. To some, it seems as if it is a game or puzzle to be figured out. Some students view mathematics as a set of arbitrary rules and procedures they need to learn. Others see it as a dreaded chore to be avoided whenever possible. To almost all elementary students, it is a subject that is associated with a textbook or workbook. Few students fully comprehend what an integral part mathematics plays in our daily lives. This Math Stretch leads students to become aware of the role of mathematics in their own daily lives and encourages them to recognize connections between the mathematics they encounter in the classroom and their real-life experiences.

Teachers have long recognized the value of making connections to improve reading comprehension. By making connections, students draw upon the background knowledge or schema they already have as they encounter new ideas, melding them together to construct meaning from what they read. During reading instruction, teachers explicitly teach students how "to access and use their prior knowledge and experiences to better understand what they read" (Harvey and Goudvis 2000). Students learn that there are three types of contextual connections they make as they read: text-to-self, text-to-text, and text-to-world.

In text-to-self connections, readers identify situations or links to their own lives in the text. This makes it easier for them to relate to the characters in a story, to visualize a scene, or in other ways connect to their reading. Text-to-text connections occur when students are able to see similarities between the text they are currently reading and another text they have read. The more reading experiences students have, the more they have to draw upon in making these connections. With text-to-world connections, students relate what they are reading to what they know about the world in general.

While one might think that these connections would occur spontaneously as students read, that's not always the case. Often, students who begin school with a rich literary background easily make these connections as they read or are read to. For these children, bedtime brought the promise of snuggling with a family member as books were read, often repeatedly reading the same story. Not only were these books shared, but they were also the starting point for conversations linking favorite stories to experiences in their own lives. Talking about the pictures in the book, the relationships between characters, or other aspects of the text expanded the horizons of these children and encouraged them to recognize connections that helped them more fully understand what they were reading.

Conversely, many children, especially those from poverty backgrounds, come to school with minimal exposure to reading.

Because they have had so few literary experiences, relating to written materials can be difficult for them. They often fail to draw upon their own experiences or emotions to help them understand the text they are reading. Frequently, the very students who if engaged in a conversation on the playground during recess would readily share connection after connection, work so hard to *read* that it doesn't even occur to them to make connections when reading. They struggle to decode word after word, rarely pausing to construct meaning from what they have read. By explicitly teaching the strategy of making connections, teachers open the door to a deep trove of personal, internal resources that students may access as they read. This improves students' reading comprehension, and as understanding increases, so does motivation and excitement about reading.

The How Did My Family Use Math Last Night? Math Stretch prompts students to use reading strategies and apply them to mathematics. For homework the night before, students are asked to record a way in which either they or family members were involved in a mathematical activity. Very young students may be asked to draw a picture to record it. Older students will write about it, perhaps in multiple ways. They might use words, number sentences, or other representations. When they arrive in the classroom, they will add their examples of how mathematics is used in our daily lives to a chart, bulletin board, or other display. The variety of responses is unlimited. They may include telling time to know when to go to bed, setting the temperature on the oven, measuring ingredients to prepare food for dinner, figuring gas mileage, balancing a checking account, figuring how much is owed on an overdue book at the library, or counting out silverware to set the table. As students see and understand the responses made by others, they will make more mathematical connections to their own real-life experiences.

Arthur Hyde, in *Comprehending Math: Adapting Reading Strategies to Teach Mathematics, K–6* (2006) modifies the three types of making connections used in reading to adapt them to math comprehension. The mathematical connections he sets forth are: Math to Self, Math to World, and Math to Math. With the How Did My Family Use Math Last Night? Math Stretch, the first two are emphasized as students reflect on and share their mathematical experiences at home and in their environments. Just as with reading instruction, effective teachers explicitly teach this comprehension strategy with mathematics so that student understanding is enriched by an awareness of the context that surrounds the concepts being studied.

When it is time to discuss this exercise, students are excited about sharing their Math-to-Self and Math-to-World connections. Later, these displays can be referred to during mathematics lessons to "build bridges from the new to the known" (Harvey and Goudvis 2000). In addition, in this stretching activity, teachers are given insight into the mathematical experiences of their students at home and in the community which, along with their experiences at school, can provide meaningful contexts for future mathematical tasks (NCTM 2000). As students become adept at making connections, their conceptual understanding increases, and with it, their ability to apply these concepts in new, unfamiliar contexts increases.

Some teachers may choose to make this a regular weekly stretch so that students form the habit of looking for mathematical connections in their home lives. Other teachers may use it when new concepts are being introduced as a way of helping students tap into their prior knowledge and experiences. In either case, it provides an opportunity to explicitly teach the strategy of making connections while at the same time actually having students apply it, thus addressing the NCTM Connections Standard (2000) which states that students will be able to "recognize and apply mathematics in contexts outside of mathematics."

_____ Makes Me Think Of... Math Stretch

As a mini-activating strategy for the introduction of a new concept, a review of a previously studied concept, or as a reflective exercise related to mathematical concepts currently being studied, students begin the day by recording a word or words that they think of when they are given a concept or a word. For example, if the class is beginning a unit on fractions, the teacher writes *Fractions make me think of...* on a large sheet of chart paper or on a whiteboard.

Students are asked to write words that come to mind as they think of fractions. Each student is expected to record a word or phrase that has not already been recorded. In this stretch activity, only words are to be used—no numerals, pictures, or other representations. In kindergarten or early first grade, however, students may draw simple pictures and label them, using their "best guess" spelling. It is important that these young students be taught exactly what a *simple* drawing is through teacher modeling prior to introducing this morning stretch. Otherwise, this activity becomes much too time consuming to use as a brief morning warm-up.

For each word posted during this stretch, another connection is being made by the students—Math to Self, Math to World, and Math to Math. In the ensuing large-group discussion, as students share what they have written and explain why they chose these words, teachers highlight the value of making these connections and encourage students to use this strategy whenever they are engaged in mathematical work. This stretch directly addresses the NCTM Connections Standard (2000) as it encourages students to recognize connections among mathematical ideas and understand how they interconnect.

The student contributions to this chart also enable teachers to gauge their background knowledge and identify any misconceptions they may have. Lessons can then be adapted to meet the specific needs of the students. The discussion may also lead some students to tap into previously unconsidered prior knowledge that was sparked by the comments of other students. The student-generated word list can remain posted in the classroom. Students can continue to add words as they think of them. If students decide that a word they posted is not really related to the given word, they may cross it out or erase it.

Planning Morning Math Stretches

These morning Math Stretches are only a few examples of the kind of activities teachers can use to motivate their students to begin thinking mathematically as the day begins. Teachers may adapt other activities to create these brief stretches. When creating Math Stretches, it is important to keep in mind the following characteristics:

- They are very brief.
- They can be completed by students independently.
- They prompt students to think mathematically.
- They generate mathematical communication.

Some teachers find it convenient to repeatedly use the same five stretches each week, assigning one regularly for each day of the week. Students come to know the schedule and what to expect as they enter the classroom. An example of a weekly plan of the morning Math Stretches for a third grade class is shown in Figure 3.2.

Figure 3.2 Morning Stretch Plan for a Week

Day of the Week	Morning Stretch	Topic
Monday	Number of the Day	180
Tuesday	What's Next?	1, 3, 9, 27, …
Wednesday	How Did My Family Use Math Last Night?	Real-life mathematical connections
Thursday	_____ Makes Me Think Of…	Multiplication
Friday	Data Collection	Where would you rather go on a field trip? • science museum • planetarium • aquarium

In this case, students know that they will encounter a Number of the Day Math Stretch every Monday morning, only the number will change from week to week. On Tuesdays, they will always work on a What's Next? Math Stretch, and so on throughout the week. Having a regular and familiar routine for morning Math Stretches allows students to know what they will be expected to do each day and be prepared for it. This also can make planning easier for the teacher.

Teachers who prefer more flexibility in planning can pick and choose stretching exercises that best meet their instructional goals. Whether used to preview a new concept, explore current areas of study, or review concepts examined earlier in the year, teachers have flexibility in designing morning Math Stretches, always keeping in mind that the goal is to provide a quick, mathematical "mind focus" as students begin each school day.

Mathematical Current Events

For many years, teachers have incorporated current events into their instruction. Even with the effects of testing mandates, most educators and the general public feel that students should receive a well-rounded education. For most, *well-rounded* means that students are informed about what is going on in the world today, along with acquiring the knowledge mandated by the state curriculum. Often, textbooks are a poor resource for teaching current events as they are out-of-date as soon as they are printed. To keep current about world news, teachers and students turn to the media. Teachers in the past frequently shared articles from newspapers or magazines with the students or required students to bring in articles of interest. Some classes subscribed to weekly news magazines. Today, teachers and students more often turn to the Internet to follow the news from around the world. Regardless of the source of information, current-events instruction is rarely included in disciplines other than social studies or science.

Although it is not frequently a point of focus in current-events instruction, mathematics is relevant in much of the news. In politics, the polls rely heavily on numbers. Understanding the state of the economy requires knowledge of math—unemployment percentages, inflation rates, the rising and falling of the stock market. Reports from wars include the numbers of casualties, costs of the conflict, or related statistics. To report on the effects of a drought, journalists rely on mathematical calculations to accompany their descriptions of conditions in the affected areas. Storm coverage includes precipitation amounts, flood levels, wind velocity, monetary damages, and numbers of people impacted. Sports coverage provides win/loss statistics, records set, averages, and salary negotiations. Tables and graphs are an integral part of news reports because they organize data in ways that are easily assimilated by the public.

Our students live in a world where current events swirl around them unceasingly. Some students are more aware of them than others. Some students are only focused on current events relevant to their own particular interests. Some students are almost completely oblivious to world events. In spite of their levels of awareness, mathematical connections are rarely, if ever, recognized. When current events are included in mathematics instruction, students become aware of the ever-present relationship of mathematics to the world around them. Mathematics becomes more meaningful and relevant, and students begin to notice how it frequently impacts their lives. As this occurs, these connections offer teachers valuable opportunities to incorporate real-life mathematical contexts into class investigations and problem-solving activities.

Mathematical current events are not difficult to include in the morning routine. Initially, the teacher posts math-related news articles on a bulletin board and discusses them with the class. He or she explains through a think-aloud the math connection and how it helps the public understand the subject of the article. The first few articles should be diverse and illustrate various ways in which mathematics relates to current events. As students begin to appreciate the role of mathematics in the news, they are asked to bring in articles to be posted and discussed. Lavishly commending students for contributing articles to the current-events board usually motivates others to do the same. If not, extra-credit may be given for articles brought in, or a homework assignment might require finding a news article and writing about the mathematical connection.

As current events are posted and analyzed for mathematical relevance, teachers can also help students discover that mathematics can be used to distort the truth at times. Students begin to appreciate the necessity of evaluating the validity of news reports as they see how numbers can be manipulated. A teacher-guided check for mathematical accuracy in news articles often brings to light incorrect data or misleading analysis and leads students to read the news, especially on the Internet, more critically.

Mathematics-Related Classroom Responsibilities

One way to bring real-life mathematical experiences to students is by involving them in classroom responsibilities that require the use of mathematics. Turning the responsibility for these tasks over to students gives them practice with daily problem solving and builds a sense of community as students work together. The tasks also have relevance to students because they can see clearly how the performance of these tasks impacts the class.

In most classrooms, there are a myriad of jobs that need to be done in the morning. Turning some of these over to designated students frees the teacher to work directly with other students who may need additional support and gives the helper students valuable mathematical experiences with authentic tasks. Initially, it takes time to identify math-related jobs that are appropriate for students to handle and to teach the students how to perform them. Patience in teaching students these tasks in the first few weeks of school pays off in the long run.

One or two students may be given responsibility for taking daily attendance. Depending on their grade level, they may only record the number of students present and the number absent. Older students may add the two numbers together to check their totals, or they may be asked to compute the percentage of students present and absent. Figuring absentee percentages is especially useful if the class sets monthly goals for attendance. Students may also be given the responsibility of determining the best way to display this data so that the entire class can follow its progress toward meeting the attendance goal. This activity gives the student helpers authentic practice in computation and data analysis while motivating all students in the class to attend school regularly.

As schools strive to maximize student achievement, many are seeking ways for students to assume greater responsibility for their own learning. Some schools encourage teachers to show students how to set their own personal goals and then self-monitor their progress toward reaching their goals. After students confer with their teachers to set their goals, they create and maintain personal, foldable booklets using graphs to document their progress. These booklets may be used to record data related to reading points or math-fact fluency, for example. To vividly show their progress, the students graph, often in bright colors, their data for each goal. As students analyze their personal data, it becomes obvious how mathematics can assist them in their efforts to meet their goals. When students set and then assume responsibility for using data to track their own progress, they learn beneficial life skills and discover the utility of mathematics.

Additional math-related tasks abound for students in classrooms. If snacks are part of the school day, student helpers may use attendance numbers to determine how many snacks will be needed that day. Fosnot and Dolk (2001) describe a preschool program in which class helpers were asked not just to determine how many snacks were needed, but whether there were enough snacks to serve one to each classmate who was present. The helpers were given sheets containing copies of the snack item on hand in the quantity available. In addition, paper, pencils, and linking cubes were available to these helpers. The actual snack items themselves were not provided because then the helpers would simply have given them out to see if there were enough. Instead, the helpers developed various strategies using the materials available to model or draw the problem mathematically. Because their task dealt with snacks and students, not just numbers, it was very real and meaningful to them. When the helpers arrived at answers, the teacher followed up with strategic questioning, prompting students to communicate the thinking behind their "mathematizing" and supporting the growth of mathematical understanding in these preschool students. This task took students far beyond mere rote counting.

Students sell school supplies in the morning to raise funds for the American Cancer Society's Relay for Life.

Teachers who are attuned to finding mathematics in day-to-day routines will have no problem involving students in worthwhile, authentic jobs where they can practice their skills and deepen their understanding of how embedded mathematics is in our lives. When students assume responsibility for math-related tasks, they become increasingly adept at applying their mathematical prowess to everyday problems and grow confident in their understanding of the mathematical concepts involved. Mathematics assumes an importance to them because it affects their own classrooms and classmates rather than being just meaningless numbers and word problems from the pages of their math books. Involving students in these classroom jobs aligns directly with the NCTM Connections Standard (2000) which states that students should be able to "recognize and apply mathematics in contexts outside of mathematics."

Calendar Board

Visitors to elementary school classrooms worldwide find versions of Calendar Boards in various colors, styles, and designs in classroom after classroom. It is not surprising because the Calendar Board is one of the most versatile teaching tools in elementary classrooms. This interactive bulletin board includes a calendar, number lines, number charts, some kind of modeling system for place value, and a variety of components that are designed to be introduced at different times during the school year to focus on a variety of mathematical concepts. These components are displayed on a brightly-colored, inviting bulletin board in front of an open area where the class can gather. The elements of the Calendar Board vary according to grade level and to the needs of the students.

Commercial daily calendar programs are available, but are not necessary. The commercial programs provide an array of preplanned and prepared activities that change from month to month and include many materials ready for use. If commercially produced programs are used, however, teachers are advised to be selective in deciding which of the components to use and when to use them. Calendar Board instruction should be designed to meet the instructional needs of students. Teachers who keep that in mind can choose which of the components meet the needs of their students and use them, not necessarily in the order suggested by the program. However, using ready-made programs can be a valuable time saver for teachers. And, as long as the ready-made programs are used to support the established instructional goals rather than guide them, they can be very effective.

The Calendar Board allows teachers to offer consistent, daily learning opportunities covering a range of mathematical concepts. During the brief fifteen minutes of the daily instructional segment, students are actively engaged in a continuous learning process as they interact with its elements. The consistency of the daily instruction helps students incrementally build understanding of mathematical "big ideas," challenges them to notice patterns and relationships, and encourages them to share their mathematical discoveries in class discussions. Daily

Calendar Board use by teachers does the following:

- gives students support in learning mathematics incrementally as they develop understanding over time
- provides visual models to help students recognize mathematical relationships
- fosters the growth of mathematical language acquisition and promotes student reasoning ability through mathematical conversations
- promotes algebraic thinking
- allows teachers to informally observe their students' mathematical understanding and then adapt instruction to meet students' needs (Gillespie and Kanter 2005)

The Calendar Board is an excellent vehicle for previewing concepts, reviewing previously mastered concepts as maintenance, and engaging students in ongoing, daily practice with concepts that are difficult to master.

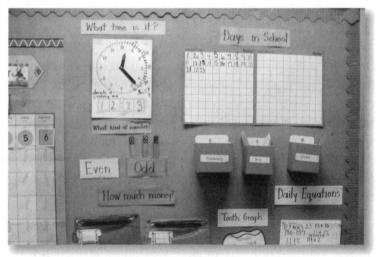

This sample Calendar Board reviews many essential mathematical concepts.

Providing some prior experience with mathematical concepts in the weeks before their presentation in a regular mathematics lesson gives students scaffolding for new learning, thereby increasing their success when they eventually work with these concepts. This instructional strategy of previewing is effective for all students, but is especially effective with struggling students who frequently bring less background knowledge to the learning experience. Research shows that the more academically-oriented experiences students have, the more opportunities they have to store those experiences as academic background knowledge upon which they can draw (Marzano 2004). Giving students opportunities to think about new knowledge before they actually experience it enhances their achievement. Previewing activates students' prior knowledge and builds additional academic background knowledge with brief, introductory tasks linked to the concepts to come. This bridges the gap between what they know and what they need to know to successfully learn and understand these concepts (Marzano, Pickering, and Pollock 2001). Calendar Board instruction provides an ideal structure for engaging students in these daily tasks a week or two before the actual unit of study when the concepts will be addressed. Furthermore, relevant vocabulary can be presented and revisited daily, leading up to the actual introduction of the concepts. When students finally encounter these concepts in greater depth, they are able to confidently make connections to their recently accumulated experiences and build on those foundations.

Once concepts have been learned, students need to continue to work with them to maintain and strengthen their understanding. The initial practice with these concepts during the unit of study is considered massed practice—practice sessions placed very close to each other during the mathematical instruction on the standards being taught. Massed practices lead to student mastery, but for deeper conceptual understanding, student work with these concepts needs to be continued at less frequent intervals (Marzano, Pickering, and Pollock 2001). This distributed practice, as it is known, is often neglected until the weeks before high-stakes testing when teachers provide intense review of the entire year's curriculum. As an alternative, the Calendar Board offers teachers a time to briefly revisit previously taught concepts and skills on a regular basis. This helps students maintain understanding and competency while freeing the regular mathematics instruction time for teaching other mathematical standards. Rather than a fever-pitch, overall review prior to testing, the ongoing revisiting promotes deeper understanding and with it, increases the ability of students to apply their knowledge to new or different contexts.

Additionally, the Calendar Board provides opportunities for year-long ongoing practice of skills with which students traditionally have difficulty. For example, second grade students often struggle with finding missing addends. Therefore, a teacher may decide that on the Calendar Board every Tuesday, he or she will present students with problems requiring them to determine missing addends. With experience, teachers are able to identify which concepts are most difficult for students to master at any given grade level. In planning for the Calendar Board, from the beginning of the year, activities related to these concepts are provided to scaffold and strengthen the conceptual understanding of students throughout the year. By consulting state standards and using their own creativity, teachers can think of many ideas to be practiced during calendar instruction.

The variety of specific elements that can be included in a Calendar Board lesson is limited only by a teacher's creativity. Often, students use the calendar to determine the date and the passage of time. In doing so, they often identify patterns the teacher creates with the daily calendar pieces. Depending on the grade level, the pieces may repeat a pattern of simple shapes and colors or can have much more complex patterns related to mathematical concepts being studied. For younger students, a discussion about seasons and weather is included.

Calendar pieces can display complex concepts, such as angle measure, or simpler concepts, such as color patterns.

Graphing activities related to real-life data collections are frequently included in Calendar Board (NCTM 2000). Throughout the year, students practice compiling different kinds of graphs and tables. The group then analyzes the data to determine trends and patterns. Topics for graphing activities that may be included can be chosen by both teachers and students. Many classes compile graphs that track birthdays or weather patterns. A class may even decide to assist the lunchroom staff by compiling data on favorite lunch selections. Using authentic scenarios helps students understand how graphing and mathematics are part of their daily lives.

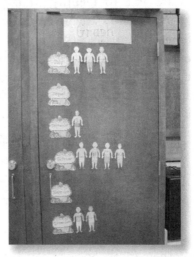

This graph displays students' birthdays.

Calendar Board elements often include *measurement* activities. They may involve determining the outdoor or indoor temperature, sorting canned food by weight, finding the circumference of pumpkins during the fall, or determining the height of students. Teachers can creatively connect measurement opportunities to other content-area units of study throughout the year, so that they are not limited solely to the few weeks of the measurement unit. These activities support the NCTM Measurement Standards, which state that students should be able to understand the measurable attributes of objects and use appropriate tools to determine measurements (2000).

This measurement activity combines mathematics and science.

To hone students' *estimation* skills, the teacher may provide weekly estimation challenges. A jar or bag of objects is shown to the class. Students estimate how many objects are in it. Or, an object may be shown to the class for students to estimate its length or weight. The repetition of these activities throughout the year allows students to develop greater proficiency at these skills than the experience they get during a unit lasting a week or two.

Estimation can be difficult for students, so it should be practiced as often as possible.

Number lines are usually created by adding a number for each day of school. Skip counting can be practiced as a group as number patterns are identified. Prediction activities are often included. At the beginning of the year, students might predict how far around the room the number line will extend by the end of the school year. Students might be given opportunities to adjust their predictions periodically during the year.

On this number line, each day is represented as .01.

The Calendar Board also provides opportunities to address *place value*. In primary classrooms, straws may represent ones and then be bundled to become tens or hundreds. In upper elementary classrooms, students work with place value for decimals or numbers of much greater magnitudes. This element of the Calendar Board, along with the previous two elements, address the NCTM Number and Operations Standard and the Representation Standard (2000).

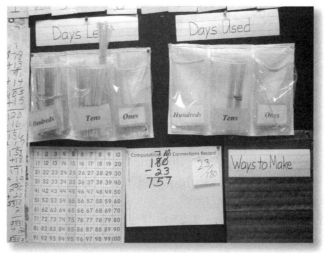

By comparing "Days left" and "Days Used" students can visualize how place value changes as numbers get larger and smaller.

Money activities are often included in the Calendar Board at some point during the year. These activities may range from simple identification of coins and their values to complex problems involving calculations of the total costs of items, the amount of change someone will receive, or calculating interest or taxes.

This activity provides students with an understanding of the relevance of mathematics in real life.

To develop students' *number sense*, the Calendar Board may include an "Incredible Equations" component. This is similar to the Number of the Day Chart used during the morning Math Stretch. A number is provided by the teacher, or students may work with the number from the day's date or the number of days they have been in school. Students suggest number sentences that equal that number. Some may be quite complex. Because of the nature of this task, students work at their own level of understanding, but may be exposed to the more complex thinking of their classmates. Students may create these equations individually or work in groups. After a number of equations have been recorded, students enjoy choosing the one they think is the "most incredible." This element of competition and fun motivates students in their explorations as they compose and decompose numbers. These activities support student understanding of the NCTM Number and Operations Standard (2000).

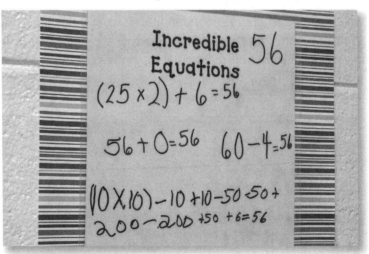

This type of activity naturally allows for differentiation in the classroom and gives students a chance to respond at their own level.

Problems of the Day (Figure 3.3) are commonly a component of Calendar Board. The teacher guides the problem-solving efforts as students tackle problems often presented in unfamiliar contexts to which they can apply mathematical skills they have already mastered. By presenting these problems in contexts that students may not be used to seeing, teachers can prepare their students to be flexible and creative in problem solving. This will help avoid the panic that sometimes occurs if students encounter contexts with which they are not familiar. These ongoing problem-solving challenges align with the NCTM Problem Solving Standard (2000). Figure 3.3 Examples of Problems of the Day

Figure 3.3 Examples of Problems of the Day

Grade Level	Problem of the Day
K–2	How many cubes do you think you can hold in one hand? Make a prediction and then find out. Work with a partner to write an addition sentence to show how many cubes you and your partner could hold altogether, each of you using only one hand.
3–5	How many three digit numbers can you think of whose digits have a product of 60 when multiplied?
6–8	The lengths of two sides of a quadrilateral are even numbers. The lengths of the other sides are odd numbers. Will the perimeter of the quadrilateral be an even or an odd number? Explain how you know.

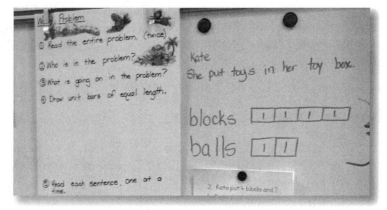

Problems of the Day allow for daily practice of problem-solving skills.

The numerous Calendar Board elements described here are used when needed. Most teachers have a few elements that are part of the Calendar Board every day. Some are addressed once or twice a week. Some are used only a few times a year. The flexibility of the Calendar Board allows the teacher to adjust the instruction based on the needs of the class.

Planning for Morning Math Warm-ups

Although the amount of time allotted to the Morning Math Warm-up is relatively minor, these routine events can have a major impact on the attitudes of students as they participate in the regular mathematics lesson later in the day. Careful planning helps students transition from the hustle and bustle of waking up, getting ready for school, and then traveling to school. As they exercise their mathematical thinking in these brief, focused activities, students are nudged toward readiness for the mathematics lesson to come.

The consistent structure of the Morning Math Warm-up components makes planning relatively simple for teachers. Teachers can choose elements from the array of components that support the learning needs of their students and address the standards they are teaching. The consistent structure also facilitates classroom management as students are taught the basic procedures for these elements at the beginning of the year. Upon entering the classroom each day, they are well aware of the expectations and can assume responsibility for carrying out the expected tasks with little direction from the teacher. The teacher can then focus on working with those students who need extra support.

Chapter Snapshot

It is important for students to prepare their minds to begin the day. Using brief Math Stretches in the morning allows students to transition from their home environments to a school environment that is centered on academics.

There are many different types of Math Stretches, and the concepts studied can vary depending on grade level and students' level of understanding. Concepts such as data analysis, geometry, and number sense can all be studied using Math Stretches. By including all students in the morning Math Stretch, they have a shared mathematical learning experience. This is important because students can refer to this shared experience during discussion in Math Huddle and this builds their background knowledge on the concepts discussed.

Calendar Board activities can be used daily to reinforce mathematical concepts that need to be covered throughout the school year. Depending on the grade level, concepts such as place value, fractions, operations, and problem solving can be covered during this instructional time. Calendar time also provides an opportunity to have a Math Huddle, where the daily Math Stretch is discussed. Math Huddle is an important time for mathematical discourse and questioning and can give teachers insight into students' understanding of the concepts that have been taught.

Review and Reflect

1. Think about how your students begin their day in your classroom. Is there a mathematical connection? Does it involve more than a worksheet?

2. Why is it important to help students recognize the links between math and their own lives? What are you doing in your classroom to help students make this connection? How can you make the link even stronger?

1 2 3
4 5 6
7 8 9

Using Guided Math with the Whole Class

Chapter one began with a description of a traditional math class in which working with the whole class was the primary mode of instruction being used for every lesson. This instructional approach has been used for as long as there have been schools. Why should we change now? Do we need to change? Is whole-class instruction the most effective instructional method?

Teachers who have been in education over the years know the cyclical nature of what are regarded as the best teaching methods. Teachers are caught in the crosswinds as educational trends come and go and then come again. We frantically work to adapt our classroom teaching methods to what must certainly be the "right" way to teach, the most effective way of reaching those students who struggle in our classes.

In our passion to reach all of our students, we grasp at the hope offered by these new approaches. As we embrace the new, we often see the value of some of the methods we have used in the past, which are being abandoned in light of the current advice of our educational leaders. Being pushed in one direction and then pulled in another, teachers can become frustrated and unsure of their capabilities.

Fortunately, many teachers trust their own instincts and experience, regularly reflecting on their teaching practices. These educators study new research in search of ways to refine their teaching methods. Joining in professional learning communities with their colleagues, they try new approaches in their classrooms, adapt them as needed, and, if effective, integrate them into their overall instructional approach without necessarily abandoning methods that have proven to be effective in the past. Their focus is on using teaching methods that work in situations where they work best.

Before discarding methods entirely in our efforts to improve our instruction, we should evaluate their effectiveness in a variety of contexts. While whole-class instruction may not be the most effective approach for *all* lessons, it can be used quite effectively for some instructional purposes.

Advantages of Whole-Class Instruction

As we know, whole-class instruction was the mainstay in schools of the past, and it still is in some classes. Any instructional method that has been used over such a long period of time by so many teachers must have some advantages, and it does. Whole-class instruction provides teachers with a quick method of presenting information to all students. Everyone receives the same information and engages in the same activity at the same time. The following list provides scenarios where whole-class instruction is appropriate:

- presenting mini lessons
- involving students in activating strategies
- reading aloud mathematics-related literature
- setting the stage for Math Workshop
- conducting a Math Huddle
- providing practice and review
- formal testing or assessments

Instructional planning is much simpler with this mode of instruction. Teachers are only required to plan one lesson at one instructional level. All students are expected to complete the same assignments. In contrast to having to plan for centers, independent student activities, and small-group instruction for several groups, planning for whole-class instruction is streamlined.

When teachers aim to capture the interest of the entire class and tap their prior knowledge as a unit of study begins, whole-class instruction can be very effective. Activating activities may be used to stimulate interest about the coming topics of study and provide the teacher with valuable insights about what students already know or misconceptions they may have. As a kick-off for a new instructional unit, whole-class instruction works effectively.

In chapter two, the importance of building a classroom learning community was emphasized. One of the ways in which a sense of community is built is through common experiences. As a class works together, common experiences are generated. Even in situations in which the class has been working in groups, coming together for mathematical conversation builds a sense of community. The participation of students in discourse concerning their mathematical ideas not only builds community, but also deepens their understanding and improves their mathematical communication skills. "Students who reflect on what they do and communicate with others about it are in the best position to build useful connections in math," according to Hiebert et al. (1997). The reflection and reasoning required for student participation in conversations about their shared mathematical experiences explicitly support the NCTM Process Standards: problem solving, reasoning and proof, communication, connections, and representation (2000).

Whole-class instruction allows teachers to spend a greater amount of time engaged in direct teaching. The direct instruction by the teacher can fill the entire math period, if desired. In contrast, with small-group instruction, the teacher is usually working directly with each group of students for only a portion of the period, and so the time spent by each student working directly with the teacher is reduced. Because the effectiveness of small-group instruction is usually greater, teachers have to carefully weigh the trade-off between increased effectiveness or greater amount of time of direct instruction.

There are times when the entire class is working at approximately the same level and the teacher may choose to use whole-class instruction. Since students' needs are similar in these situations, the instruction may not have to be differentiated. Frequently, in these cases, the instruction is a review of a previously-mastered concept—perhaps just to ensure it is maintained, to prepare for a class assessment, or to prepare for high-stakes testing. This general review helps teachers discover students who may need additional help to be successful.

Challenges of Whole-Class Instruction

In spite of these benefits, many teachers find whole-class instruction to be frustrating as they struggle to meet the needs of their students. It is rare that all of the students in a class are at the same level of competency. Even experienced teachers using whole-class instruction often find that the lesson goes over the heads of some students, leading to passivity and lack of attention, while failing to challenge others, leading to boredom. At best, only a part of the class may be fully engaged.

No matter how proficient a teacher may be, it is difficult to ensure that all students are attentive and academically engaged during whole-class instruction. The more time teachers spend in classrooms, the more apparent it becomes that children are easily distracted. Even when most students are actively involved in a lesson, some of them miss key instructional content while intently examining something in their desks, gazing out the window, or trying to gain the attention of nearby students.

The NCTM standards include both content and mathematics process standards (2000). To adequately address the process standards (problem solving, reasoning and proof, communication, connections, and representation), students need to be involved in mathematical conversations pertaining to their work on a regular basis. With whole-class instruction, student communication is limited. In most cases, it is dominated by the teacher as he or she informs and then questions students. True conversation between students where one's mathematical ideas are shared, reflected on, and debated is not the norm.

While teachers can effectively encourage a class discussion of shared mathematical experiences in a whole-class setting, other modes of instruction may offer better opportunities to develop these skills. As students are working on mathematical problem-solving tasks in small-group instruction, teachers are able to guide discussion and ensure that each student participates in the conversation. In large groups, it is virtually impossible for teachers to be so intimately involved. As Fountas and Pinnell (2001) describe it, large-group instruction "tends to marginalize those students who need more interaction and closer contact with the teacher…"

Research has shown the effectiveness of giving students specific descriptive feedback. Researcher John Hattie emphatically states, "The most powerful single modification that enhances achievement is feedback. The simplest prescription for improving education must be 'dollops of feedback'" (Hattie 1992). When teachers choose to use whole-class instruction, the "dollop" of descriptive feedback they are able to provide is extremely small.

Even when students are involved in independent practice as the teacher circulates around the room checking their work, the amount of time available makes the feedback to students very brief. Marzano, Pickering, and Pollock (2001) suggest that to maximize student achievement, the feedback to students should be specific as to what in their work is accurate and what isn't, and then students should be encouraged to continue working on a task until they succeed. Because of the nature of whole-class instruction, teachers may not be able to provide the quality and quantity of student-specific feedback that is necessary to maximize student achievement.

In addition, there are always some students who did not quite understand the lesson and who diligently completed their assigned tasks incorrectly. Because of the large number of students and time limits, the teacher may or may not get to these students during the independent practice. If the teacher does have opportunities to confer with them, it is often difficult to get them to modify their work once they have practiced using incorrect methods. If the work of these students is not checked during the independent practice time, their misconceptions remain and become even more deeply ingrained.

Related to the challenges stated in the preceding paragraphs is assessment. In recent years, teachers have become increasingly aware of the importance of assessment, both summative and formative. Summative assessment, which is more evaluative in nature, allows teachers to see exactly what students have achieved after a unit or units of study. Summative assessments are designed to be large-scale assessments of learning. Formative assessment, on the other hand, is an ongoing assessment used to inform daily instruction. Formative assessments are assessments for learning. These day-to-day informal assessments provide immediate, accurate evidence of student learning. The results help teachers to make the crucial instructional decisions that affect the future content being taught.

According to Stiggins (2004), the use of assessments for learning has been shown to trigger remarkable gains in student learning. Assessments "provide a continuous flow of evidence of student mastery of classroom-level learning targets that lead over time to attainment of the desired achievement standards." Working with students in small groups and conferring individually with them lets teachers gauge the level of learning and then adjust instruction accordingly. Moreover, teachers are able to teach students to assess their own learning using rubrics and other assessment tools. Once students learn to determine their levels of mastery, teachers show them how to set learning goals and later how to monitor their progress toward reaching their goals.

Since the majority of these ongoing assessments for learning are based on observing students, listening to students talk and engaging them in conversations, and reviewing the quality of the students' work products, they are difficult to do well with whole-class instruction. Instead of the informal assessments described, teachers turn to short paper-and-pencil assessments. These, for the most part, assess outcomes rather than the thought processes leading to these outcomes. While these assessments may provide a glimpse into the degree of student learning, they fail to provide information about the complexities underlying the concepts of student understanding and mastery. Without this additional information, the value of using these assessments for planning instruction is limited.

Whole-class instruction is only one of the tools available to teachers as they plan their instruction. Teachers should make use of it only for appropriate instructional tasks.

Mini Lessons

For setting the tone and introducing the concepts to be explored in a lesson, teachers often choose to present a brief mini lesson at the beginning of a class using whole-class instruction. As a way of summing up the activities students have been engaged in during a lesson, teachers may also conduct a mini lesson to summarize the learning that took place. These lessons directly instruct students on a skill, strategy, or mathematical understanding that they can use with their mathematical explorations or problem-solving tasks.

Ideally, students spend most of their math class engaged in mathematical exploration, problem solving, and mathematical discourse to develop their conceptual understanding. Mini lessons are primarily teacher directed and are valuable, but should be brief, yet explicit—no more than ten minutes. Teachers who clearly identify the teaching point of the lesson and thoughtfully plan how to present it in those few minutes are able to focus student attention in much the same way as teachers who conduct mini lessons prior to writing workshops. In fact, the "architecture" Lucy Calkins (2000) describes for writing mini lessons provides an excellent framework for mathematics mini lessons (Figure 4.1).

Figure 4.1 Architecture of a Math Mini Lesson

Architecture of a Mathematics Mini Lesson	
Connection	• With yesterday's lesson • With the ongoing unit of study • With students' work • With an experience outside of school
Teaching Point	• Present verbally • Demonstrate or model
Active Engagement	• Students try out a skill or strategy • Students act like researchers as they watch a demonstration • Students plan their work out loud • Students imagine trying a skill or strategy
Link to Ongoing Student Work	• Students turn to their own work and apply the teaching point

(Adapted from *Growing Readers: Units of Study in the Primary Classroom* by Kathy Collins, 2004.)

Connection

Calkins (2000) suggests that teachers begin mini lessons by making a connection to what students have learned in earlier lessons or to students' real-life experiences out of school. By tapping into their prior knowledge, teachers generate student interest and prepare them for the new ideas to be presented.

Teaching Point

The teacher states the teaching point very clearly by saying, "Today I am going to teach you…" More than just telling, though, the teacher demonstrates and models the strategies or concepts that he or she wants students to learn. The teacher alerts students to particularly important aspects of the demonstration or modeling by saying, "Please pay close attention to…" or "Notice how I…" Teachers think aloud, describing their thought process and the strategies they may be using. Explicitly demonstrating or modeling the use of mathematical strategies and mathematical language gives students a broad foundation upon which they can base their independent work later in Math Workshop.

Active Engagement

Before students are expected to apply the teaching point in their independent work, they are given an opportunity to try it out in very brief guided practice. This gives the teacher a way to determine how well students understand the teaching point and to reinforce student learning through guided practice (Pearson and Gallagher 1983). It is important that teachers devise ways to provide active engagement for students that do not require large amounts of time. Teachers may use "turn-and-talk" where a student turns to a specified partner or to the student seated closest to him or her as a way of encouraging active engagement by their students. During this time, students may be asked to restate the teaching point in their own words, tell how they will apply the demonstrated strategy, or use individual whiteboards to show how a procedure or strategy is used.

Link to Ongoing Work

The final component of the mini lesson is to link the teaching point to ongoing student work. Before the conclusion of the mini lesson, students are reminded that the teaching point is something that they should remember and use whenever appropriate, whether engaged in mathematics at school or at home. Students are also reminded that thoughtful mathematicians consider the possible strategies they may use and then apply only those that will help them solve the problems they are working on. The link is simply a quick and to-the-point reminder for students of the connection of the teaching point to their mathematical explorations and problem-solving activities.

Sample Mini Lesson

The following is an example of what a teacher might say in a mini lesson that teaches students how to use drawings to help visualize a problem. The application of this reading comprehension strategy to mathematical problem solving is appropriate for any grade level, although the problems to be solved will vary from grade level to grade level.

Connection: *Mathematicians, you are getting to be such good problem solvers. It's exciting to see how you approach solving problems. We talked earlier about how we can find things in math problems to which we can connect. As we have worked together in small groups to solve problems, I have heard you talk about connections you have made. Today, I am going to teach you another strategy that mathematicians use when they are trying to solve a problem.*

Teaching Point: *When mathematicians have to solve problems, they know how important it is to be able to picture or visualize them. If I can actually picture what is happening in a problem, it makes it easier for me to solve. It's kind of like a movie in my mind. When I have a problem to solve, sometimes I draw a picture of it.*

Today, I brought cookies for the class to celebrate the completion of our class book. The recipe I used made three-dozen cookies. Will I have enough cookies? Will there be leftovers? If so, what shall I do with them?

Let's see what I know so I can picture it. I know that a dozen is twelve. So I'm going to draw twelve cookies. (Draw 12 circles on the board to represent a dozen cookies.) Notice how I take the information from the problem and draw it. Now I've drawn one dozen circles to stand for the dozen cookies, but my recipe made three dozen. I'm going to draw two dozen more cookies. (Draw 24 more circles on the board to represent two dozen more cookies.) *To help me picture how many I have altogether, I'm going to circle groups of ten so I can figure out exactly how many I have.* (Circle groups of ten circles.) *Okay, that's three groups of ten and six ones—36. We have 20 students in our class—and me, of course. That makes 21 people. So I should have enough cookies since 36 is greater than 21. But, I also wanted to know how many would be left. I'm going to draw happy faces to show the cookies that we will eat. Twenty-one is 2 tens and 1 one. Let's see—I'm drawing a big happy face on 2 tens.* (Draw happy faces on two groups of 10 circles.) *Then, I'm drawing a happy face on 1 one.* (Draw a happy face on one additional circle.) *So, I have 1 ten and 5 ones left. That's 15.*

Did you notice how I drew a picture to show me what the problem was about? Drawing a picture really helped me see what was going on in that problem. When you need to understand a problem, it helps to try to visualize it. Drawing a picture is one way of being able to "see" what's going on.

Active Engagement: *Now, I want you to try to help me solve the rest of my problem. What shall we do with the leftover cookies? We found that 15 cookies will be left. Please use your whiteboards. Draw the cookies that will be left. Show what you think we should do with them.* (Give students time to draw the cookies and show what they will do with them.) *Now, turn to your partner and tell him or her what you would do with the leftover cookies.* (Give students time to discuss with their partners.)

You drew the leftover cookies to show exactly how many there were and then showed what you would do with them. I heard many interesting ideas for what to do with the cookies. By picturing what was going on in the problem, it was easier to solve it.

Link: *So, mathematicians, remember that when you are trying to solve a problem, whether it is one here at school or one you face at home, it often helps to visualize it by drawing a picture of what's happening. As we work today, I am going to be looking to see who is using this strategy for problem solving.*

Tips for Effective Mini Lessons

To make the most of mini lessons, Collins (2004) makes several recommendations. These recommendations have been slightly adapted to fit mathematical mini lessons.

- **Limit student talk.** While mathematical discourse is an integral part of mathematics instruction, the mini lesson is not the place for it. The amount of student talk should be guided and controlled.

- **Keep the connection brief.** Avoid the temptation to ask questions to make the mathematical connection. Frequently, in trying to access prior knowledge and reminding the class of previous lessons, teachers will question students. Rather than drawing out the mini lesson with extensive questioning, the teacher can simply remind the class of what has already been learned.

- **State the teaching point simply and reiterate it.** Avoid over-explaining the mathematics teaching point, but repeat it often during the mini lesson. Many mathematical concepts will take students a while to deeply understand.

- **Demonstrate the mathematics teaching point.** Show, model, and use think-alouds to help students understand the mathematics teaching point.

- **Use a familiar context for problem solving.** If the context is familiar to students, they can concentrate on the mathematics teaching point itself instead of having to concentrate on understanding the context of the problem.

- **Match the active engagement to the mathematics teaching point.** The goal of the active engagement component is to involve students in using the mathematics teaching point.

Activating Strategies

Research has consistently shown that activating prior knowledge is critical to students' learning (Marzano, Pickering, and Pollock 2001). Just as reading comprehension involves both conscious and unconscious strategies to access, use, and modify the prior knowledge of the reader, those involved in mathematical activities are engaged in a similar, complex process as they seek to understand and solve problems. The connections students make with their own individual sets of knowledge make it possible for them to engage in higher-level comprehension strategies (Fountas and Pinnell 2001).

In addition to establishing links to the prior knowledge of students, teachers can enhance learning by helping students anticipate the new knowledge to be introduced. Activating strategies used at the beginning of a unit of study offer students insight into information to be introduced. These cognitive activating strategies are not summaries or overviews, but are scaffolding that bridges the gap between the prior knowledge of the learners and what they need to know to be successful with the new concepts they will learn. Previewing key vocabulary prepares students for concepts to come. Some teachers present a concept map of the upcoming unit or build a foundation for learning by creating a new experience for students that acts as a hook to stimulate their interest (Thompson and Thompson 2005). These motivational peeks at "coming attractions" may be achieved through the use of a variety of techniques.

KWL Charts

One of the most frequently used activating strategy is a KWL chart. (See Figure 4.2 on the following page.) This type of chart leads students to recall knowledge they already have about a given topic, to consider what they would like to learn about it, and then reflect on what they have learned once the topic is taught. Not only does this organizer generate students' background knowledge, but it also gives direction to student learning by having them list things they want to learn. Teachers learn about the knowledge and misconceptions of their students as they complete a class KWL chart.

The organizer itself consists of three columns. The first column is generally titled "Things I Know." In many cases, what students think they know may not actually be true, so it may be best to label it *K— Things I Think I Know*. Throughout the unit, the class may return to the chart and revise it as they find errors in what they thought they knew. The second column is titled *W—Things I Want to Know,* and the third column is titled *L—Things I Learned.*

Figure 4.2 KWL Chart

K Things I Think I Know	W Things I Want to Know	L Things I Learned

To use this chart as an activating strategy, the teacher introduces the upcoming unit and encourages students to think about what they already know (the link to prior knowledge). The teacher enters their responses in the left-hand column. Older students may have their own individual copies on which they can record their responses. Then the class brainstorms questions they have about the topic (the hook to motivate learning), and the teacher records them. The chart hangs in the classroom to be referred to as a reminder to the class of what they want to learn as the unit of study progresses. At various times during the unit, the class may add questions or begin to fill in the third column with things they have learned. Finally, the chart serves as a review tool after the unit ends and students have completed the third column with information that they have learned.

Hyde, in his book *Comprehending Math: Adapting Reading Strategies to Teach Mathematics, Grades K–6* (2006), adapts the KWL chart for use in problem solving. In many ways, an activating strategy serves the same purposes when trying to understand a mathematical problem as it does as preparation for a new unit. The first column in Hyde's chart becomes, *What do you know for sure?* Here students may add both prior knowledge they have that may be connected to the problem and also the facts from the problem itself. The second column becomes, *What are you trying to find out?* In this column, students record what they need to figure out or find to solve the problem. Answering this question focuses students on the relevant issues in the problem. The third column becomes, *Are there any special conditions in the problem?*, which is often the most difficult for students to determine. Using this chart helps students blend their own knowledge with what they learn from the problem and then highlights and clarifies their task in solving the problem.

Anticipation Guides

An anticipation guide (See Figure 4.3 on the following page.) is a set of questions about the concepts in a coming unit which students are asked to answer based on their background knowledge and experiences at the beginning of the unit. Students begin to make connections and wonder about the content in the upcoming unit as they work to answer the questions. If students have not worked with anticipation guides previously, teachers should reassure students that they are not expected to be able to answer all of the questions, but to do the best they can. Highly motivated students may be upset initially if they don't know the answers. By explaining the purpose of the guide, student concerns may be avoided. At the conclusion of the unit, students enjoy returning to the anticipation guide to see how much they have learned. In addition, it can help students become aware of any confusion or misunderstandings they may still have so that they can be addressed.

Sample Anticipation Guide for Decimal and Percent Concepts

Decide whether each statement is true or false and mark your answer in the column marked *Before*. Once the unit of study is finished, read each statement again. Decide whether each statement is true or false and mark your answer in the column marked *After*. Did any of your choices change?

Figure 4.3 Anticipation Guide

Before	After	Statement
		1. Multiplication and division of two numbers will produce the same digits, regardless of the position of the decimal point.
		2. The position to the left of the decimal point is the position of the tenths.
		3. The term *percent* is simply another name for hundredths.
		4. 3/4 is equal to 0.75.
		5. If a book originally costs $10.00 and is on sale at 25% off, it will now cost $8.00.
		6. The sum of 0.25 and 0.25 is 0.5.

To prepare an anticipation guide, a teacher chooses the most important concepts to be presented in the new unit and creates up to ten statements related to the concepts. Some of these statements will be true, and some false. To generate student interest, the statements may be controversial or contrary to what a student might believe. To introduce the unit, students are asked to complete the anticipation guide either individually or in small groups. As they try to determine whether the statements are true or false, students become aware of their uncertainties and gaps in their knowledge. Teachers remind them that throughout the unit they should be looking for information to determine the validity of the statements. The guides are saved and at the end of the unit, students complete them again. Following the second completion of the guides, students discuss their answers, explaining why they chose them. If students still have incorrect answers, teachers can go back over the standards that were not completely understood with only the students who need additional help. This ensures the students' achievement and does not include students who have already mastered the concepts.

Word Splashes

A word splash is a way in which students preview unfamiliar vocabulary from an upcoming unit while building links to prior knowledge and creating hooks that will motivate their learning. To create a word splash, teachers review the standards included in the upcoming unit of study, identifying relevant and catchy vocabulary. Once the pertinent vocabulary is chosen, the words are presented to students all at once, "splashed" across a chart, transparency, or on an interactive whiteboard.

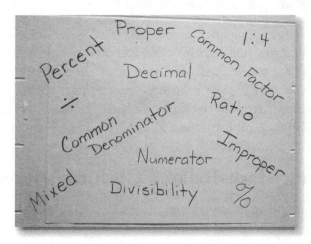

This word splash previews vocabulary for converting fractions, decimals, and percents.

As a class, students read the words and brainstorm to determine the relationship between the given words using their prior knowledge of the words and what they know about the coming unit of study. Some teachers have students write predictions as to the meaning of each word within the context of the new unit. However, it is recommended that the correct meaning of the words be provided to students during the word splash since students (and people, in general) tend to remember the first thing that they hear whether it is true or not. Rather than have students mentally maintain an erroneous meaning of a vocabulary word for a period of days, it is far better to assist students in learning the correct meanings of the words as the word splash is discussed. During the word splash, students are challenged to predict how the vocabulary words are related—why did the teacher choose those particular words for the word splash? As the unit progresses, they are encouraged to check the accuracy of their predictions as a motivation to pay close attention to the new concepts being introduced.

Alternatively, toward the end of a unit, students may be asked to create their own word splashes as a way of summarizing the content of the unit. Their choice of words allows teachers to informally assess student understanding of the new concepts. With the specific information about their students, teachers can modify instruction to ensure that every student is successful.

KWL charts, anticipation guides, and word splashes are but a few of the possible activating strategies that can be used at the beginning of a unit with the whole class since little or no differentiation is needed with these activities. The purposes—previewing vocabulary, linking to prior knowledge, and hooking student interest—lend themselves well to this mode of instruction.

Reading Math-Related Children's Literature

Students are naturally drawn to good stories, whether they are told by a teacher about his or her own life or a story read aloud. Stories make ordinary situations come alive for students. They make fantasy seem real. Many teachers use stories in their classrooms to inspire, motivate, and teach students. So, it's not at all surprising that literature is very effective when used as a vehicle for teaching mathematical concepts to students.

The use of children's literature to teach mathematical concepts is not a new idea. For many years, teachers have garnered student interest by linking a mathematical concept to an event in an engaging piece of literature. Through the story situations and the actions of the characters who populate the stories, students learn about mathematical concepts and their application (O'Connell 2007a).

Because students become thoroughly engaged in stories, math problems or concepts related to stories are almost as relevant to them as mathematical links to their real lives. And, in some cases, the contexts are much more entertaining. One of the most well-known stories used to teach subtraction of money is *Alexander Who Used to Be Rich Last Sunday* by Judith Viorst (1988). Students can identify with poor Alexander whose money slowly disappears throughout the week through a combination of unwise expenditures and misfortune. Depending on the grade level and capability of students, they can either use coins to replicate Alexander's steady loss of money or they can subtract as the story proceeds. What student has not been in a similar situation?

Viorst surely intended this book to reflect common childhood experiences in an entertaining way rather than intending that it be used to teach mathematics. However, teachers can take advantage of students' affinity for stories by establishing connections between mathematics and the stories their students read or the stories they read to their students. Just as mathematics is found in almost all aspects of our lives, mathematical links can be identified in most stories. Capitalizing on these links, teachers can teach mathematics during language arts instruction or language arts during mathematics instruction. The integration of disciplines reinforces the message that mathematics is a part of our lives, not an isolated subject only directly linked to the textbook. Using links to literature strongly supports the NCTM Connection Standards (2000) stating that students should be able to "recognize and apply mathematics in contexts outside of mathematics."

To encourage students to recognize these literature/math links, teachers can use a think-aloud strategy as they read a story, detailing the mathematical connections and questions that occur to them as they read the story. Over time, the responsibility for finding these mathematical connections can be turned over to students, who are asked to find the math in stories. As students make these mathematical links, they are also held accountable to the text and stories themselves. According to Hyde (2006), "It is the responsibility of the teacher to help students see and experience the interrelation of mathematical topics, the relationships between mathematics and other subjects, and the way mathematics is embedded in the students' world." The use of literature is an effective method with which teachers can promote understanding of those relationships.

Using mathematical language to describe connections, students learn to describe exactly what in the text was mathematics-related. Through the use of literature, teacher think-alouds, and student discussion, students become fluent with new mathematical vocabulary. Introducing mathematical language in context is the optimal way to promote the vocabulary development of students (O'Connell 2007a). Their participation in these conversations reinforces the NCTM Communication Standard (2000), which states that students should be able to "communicate their mathematical thinking coherently and clearly to peers, teachers, and others." In addition, the accountability to the text strengthens their reading comprehension skills—an essential skill for many problem-solving activities.

Over time, as the value of this math-language arts linkage became apparent, authors began writing children's literature specifically designed to teach mathematical concepts, as well as to entertain. These authors supply teachers with rich sources of instructional materials that involve students in mathematical sense-making and problem-solving activities in a nonthreatening environment (Whitin and Whitin 2000).

Whole-class instruction often proves to be the most efficient way to share rich mathematics-related literature with a class. If the teacher chooses to do a think-aloud as a book is read, the whole class is guided through the thought process as well. The follow-up discussions and activities that build on the initial read-aloud may be completed as a whole group, in small groups, or as part of Math Workshop.

Setting the Stage for Math Workshop

A visitor to a class engaged in a well-planned Math Workshop may be forgiven for failing to understand the considerable effort that goes into putting the structures and procedures in place that make it all possible. In chapter six, these will be examined more closely. However, any description of effective uses of whole-class instruction should include creating a classroom community, teaching procedures, and the ongoing need to provide directions— all necessary in setting the stage for Math Workshop.

During the first few weeks of school each year, students learn the basic procedures that make Math Workshop possible within a classroom. Most often, teachers work with the entire class in creating these procedures and teaching them. Going through this process creates shared student experiences, which in turn promote a true sense of community. As the class comes together as a community, students begin to respect the rules established and to function within this framework. It is difficult to envision this process of community building with any mode of instruction other than whole class.

Although the initial community building ends after a few weeks, it is usually necessary to revisit this process periodically throughout the year when students begin to get lax about following classroom guidelines. Teachers may choose to call the class together to regroup and re-establish its sense of community. Having the class meet as a large group can also be used to address specific problems that have arisen during mathematics instruction. The class as a whole discusses the problems and works together to solve them.

Any time students are engaged in independent mathematical work, whether they are working in a group, in pairs, or individually, their directions must be very clear. If all students are to be involved in the same work, it is most efficient to give directions to the whole class at one time. Group work is valuable, but a teacher's time is wasted if it is spent repeating the same instructions with group after group. Using whole-class instruction as an introduction to Math Workshop ensures a smooth transition into these independent activities.

Math Huddle

To promote conceptual understanding, students engage not only in mathematical activities and investigations, but also in mathematical discourse following this work. To engage students in this type of discussion, teachers can choose to have their students gather together for a Math Huddle. This concept has been called other names by other authors, such as Math Congress (Fosnot and Dolk 2001), but in my classroom, we call it Math Huddle. A Math Huddle is a forum for students to "communicate their ideas, solutions, problems, proofs, and conjectures with one another."

In contrast to a more traditional instruction model where students are simply recipients of knowledge dispensed by their teachers, in a Math Huddle, students are held accountable for expressing their ideas, for listening thoughtfully to each other, and for justifying their mathematical thinking based on their mathematical experiences. Student interactions in which they "propose mathematical ideas and conjectures, learn to evaluate their own thinking and that of others, and develop mathematical reasoning skills" enhance conceptual understanding (NCTM 2000).

Students who are involved in the process of constructing mathematical ideas are usually eager to share their ideas with others. Mathematical language gives them a vehicle through which they can represent their thoughts accurately to their peers. Eventually this language actually serves not only as a method of communication, but also as a tool for thought (Fosnot and Dolk 2001). The very process of reflection, then stating ideas, and finally, receiving feedback on those ideas, helps students fine-tune their mathematical understanding.

Conversations during a Math Huddle spur students to stretch their thinking beyond their initial ideas as they revise, refine, and test mathematical conjectures (Schultz-Ferrell, Hammond, and Robles 2007). Students are encouraged to listen intently and respectfully ask questions of their peers. The teacher acts as a facilitator, maintaining a focus on the thinking and reasoning processes of the students.

As students discuss their observations, reflections, and conjectures, misconceptions sometimes become apparent. Teachers can lead their classes to view these misconceptions as learning opportunities to be explored rather than as failures. A respectful discussion of these misconceptions maximizes the learning of the entire class since mistakes are an integral part of the process of improving methods of solving problems and of constructing understanding. As teachers summarize the learning resulting from these misconceptions, they promote a classroom culture where mistakes are recognized as being a natural part of learning. When students come to understand this, they become willing to take risks and share their ideas without fear of ridicule or censure (Hiebert et al. 1997).

Practice and Review Sessions

Throughout the year, students are involved in a process of learning, practicing, and reviewing in order to refine, extend, and then maintain the initial learning. While practice and review may be conducted in any component of Guided Math, one very effective mode of instruction for this purpose is whole-class instruction.

Pencil-and-Paper Tasks

As students develop mathematical prowess, they need opportunities to firm up their initial understandings with more coherent and delineated conceptual understandings. In traditional classroom settings, the practice and review opportunities are most often paper-and-pencil tasks. There are certainly times when teachers may want to employ them. Most high-stakes state assessments are paper-and-pencil tests. Students should be provided with some opportunities to practice using the same format that they will face during the "big" test. These can efficiently be completed in a whole-class setting.

Games and Music

More productive, however, are activities that motivate and engage students through games, music, or physical movement. While some games are more appropriate for Math Workshop, many allow a class to be divided into groups to compete. Competing in mathematical-related games motivates students to repeatedly practice mathematical skills, something that would normally be considered a chore. Work becomes play. That may be why Marzano and Pickering (2005) include student participation in games as step six in their six-step plan for building academic vocabulary. However, games are not only effective in building vocabulary, but also for building mathematical knowledge.

Teachers can create games based on the specific skills students are learning or have learned. One of these academic games can be played like *Jeopardy*®. Teachers prepare answers; students must supply the questions. To review fact families, groups of four students can compete to see which group can correctly write the facts in a fact family when they are given the numbers in the family.

To reinforce mental math skills, classes can play "Around the World." Students are seated at their desks. Two students who sit side by side stand and are given a problem to solve. The first one to answer correctly moves on to the next desk and competes against that student. The other student sits down at the desk where he or she is. The student who is the first to answer correctly continues to move from desk to desk, competing with student after student until he or she is defeated or until all students have played.

To play the "fly swatter" game, the class is divided into two teams. One representative from each team comes to the front of the room.

Each child is given a fly swatter. Answers and nonanswers to a series of questions are posted in front of the competitors. When given a question, the first student to swat the correct answer earns a point for his or her team. The content of the questions is determined by teachers to reinforce or review math skills and knowledge based on the needs of their classes.

Teachers who are fortunate enough to have an interactive whiteboard or a method of displaying *PowerPoint*® presentations are able to create the games using these technologies or to download games that have been created and shared on the Internet.

This student is using an interactive whiteboard to play a game that reviews mathematical concepts being taught in class.

Songs that teach mathematical concepts are readily available, often with a math textbook series. Younger students love to join in singing simple songs accompanied by movement. Older students enjoy raps accompanied by dance moves, which teach the basic math facts. The use of music and dance to reinforce mathematical understanding is uniquely suited to whole-class instruction where students can participate, interact with their classmates, and enjoy these activities.

Technology

Technology allows teachers to review and accurately monitor student understanding through the use of "clickers" or classroom response systems. During whole-class review sessions, each student indicates his or her responses to questions using this device. The answers are tallied and sometimes presented in graphic formats. Teachers are able to determine the overall level of understanding of the class and address misconceptions. In addition, these systems, when assigned to specific students, allow the teacher to monitor the response of each student individually. Using this data, teachers can effectively target their instruction for these students.

Assessment

One essential component of mathematics instruction is assessment. It serves evaluative purposes to determine whether students have mastered the standards. Assessment provides teachers with the information they need to tailor their instruction to meet the needs of their classes and their individual students. Using a variety of assessment methods provides teachers with an accurate view of student achievement rather than repeatedly using the same type of assessment. Assessment will be addressed more thoroughly in chapter eight.

One method of assessment, which is used perhaps more frequently than any other, is the paper-and-pencil test. Sometimes, it is formatted as a multiple-choice test, and sometimes, it is formatted as a constructed-response test. Unless a student needs a specified accommodation, testing of this kind can effectively and efficiently be administered in a whole-class setting. Scheduling small-group instruction is not easy. Instructional time is limited and should be used for activities that can have the most value and impact. In most situations, it is better to avoid wasting limited instructional time when the teacher's primary role is monitoring the students who are taking the test.

Chapter Snapshot

As teachers plan their mathematics instruction for the week, the primary focus is on the standards to be learned and the needs of the students as identified through both informal and formal assessments. With the curriculum and student needs in mind, teachers can pick and choose between the components of Guided Math, matching instructional tasks with the most effective and efficient modes of instruction.

Whole-class instruction is largely teacher-directed. All students are engaged in the same tasks with little or no variation. For those tasks that require little differentiation, whole-class instruction is an option to be considered—perhaps for the entire class period, or perhaps for only a portion of the period. Mini lessons, read-alouds, activating strategies, Math Huddles, practice-and-review sessions, and testing are ideal tasks for whole-group instruction. However, these are only suggested activities for whole-class instruction. Teachers may find times when they will use other components for these tasks, or they may find other activities that work well with whole-class instruction.

Using the Guided Math framework does not require that all instructional time is spent in any one instructional mode. It provides the flexibility and guidance to help teachers determine how to use instructional time most effectively to meet the learning needs of their students. With experience, teachers become adept at matching the curriculum and student needs with the components of Guided Math.

Review and Reflect

1. Think back to the previous week of mathematics instruction in your classroom. How much of the instruction was whole class? Why did you choose that instructional method?

2. In which situations do you use whole-class instruction most frequently? How effective is it in those situations?

1 2 3
4 **5** 6
7 8 9

Using Guided Math with Small Groups

Debbie Miller in her book *Teaching with Intention* (2008) writes of creating "the luscious feeling of endless time" in classrooms. While recognizing the enormous pressures teachers face daily, she warns of "getting done" taking precedence over "doing," and of "finishing" becoming more important than "figuring out." She writes, "When kids are given time to puzzle through something that's challenging (with just enough support from their teachers to be successful), they're not only learning about the task at hand, they're learning about who they are and how they go about figuring things out. They're developing those can-do, let-me-have-at-it attitudes that we want so much for them."

Although Miller writes about reading instruction, we want these same things for our students as they learn mathematics. In spite of time constraints, which often lead teachers to emphasize procedural fluency over conceptual understanding and to use worksheets rather than problem-solving activities, we want more for our students. We want to give them that "luscious feeling of endless time" as they ponder problems and share ideas. We want to have time to work with our struggling students and to scaffold their learning. We want to challenge those students who demonstrate their understanding quickly and are ready to move on. We want each and every student to feel challenged, and yet supported, in their mathematical learning.

How can we achieve this? Of the limited number of hours teachers have with their students each day, only a certain amount of time is scheduled for mathematics instruction. When most of this time is allocated to whole-class instruction, even teachers who recognize that children learn best when they are able to work with manipulatives, struggle to find the time in their daily lessons. Distributing to and then collecting manipulatives from an entire class requires time. Monitoring their use in a large group is also difficult. Allowing students to choose the kinds of manipulatives they will use for problem solving is avoided because it simply takes too much time.

Working with small groups, a teacher's ultimate goal is to lead students to develop conceptual understanding and have "toolboxes" of effective strategies they can draw upon to navigate independently in the world of mathematics. The teacher works with a small group of students who have similar instructional needs. In a brief mini lesson, information about a concept or strategy is shared, and then students are engaged in an activity or task practicing what has been shared. The practice work should be just beyond what the students can do independently, requiring them to stretch to be successful. The teacher provides only enough scaffolding, or support, to move the students to a higher level of competence where they can work independently. Sometimes, the tasks themselves require students to work through processes that increase their understanding. Sometimes, teacher questioning leads students to consider aspects of their tasks not previously considered. At other times, teachers facilitate interactions between students in the group that move those students to a higher level of understanding. Most importantly, students are active participants working with and exploring mathematics with an abundance of math talk throughout most of the small-group lesson. Just as children learn to read by reading, children learn mathematics by doing mathematics.

Advantages of Small-Group Instruction

In classrooms throughout the country, teachers are examining and adjusting their teaching practices, trying to create the "luscious feeling of endless time" that Miller describes (2002). Many teachers who have used Guided Reading successfully with their students are discovering the advantages of small-group mathematics instruction. By flexibly grouping students based on their strengths and needs, teachers can tailor their teaching to provide the specific instruction that best challenges all learners. Without the stress of whole-class instruction, teachers can essentially slow down and savor the feeling of "endless time" as they work with their students. Instruction is focused, materials are easily managed, conversation flows freely, and student efforts are easily monitored. Students receive the support that they need to expand their conceptual understanding and improve their procedural fluency as instruction is differentiated. As Fountas and Pinnell (2001) describe it, "In the comfort and safety of a small group, students learn how to work with others, how to attend to shared information, and how to ask questions or ask for help." These abilities are as valuable in mathematics as they are in reading.

In fact, in her writings on differentiation, Carol Ann Tomlinson suggests that teachers can challenge all learners by providing instruction at varied levels of difficulty, with scaffolding based on needs, and with time variations by using multiple instructional groups (2000). In these small instructional groups, the process, the product, and the content of learning may vary. Even the learning environment can be adjusted. While some students may need the structure of working at a table, another group may do well in less formal ways, perhaps working with manipulatives on the floor. As teachers learn to recognize the learning styles of their students, they are able to adjust instruction to maximize learning.

Because of the flexibility and fluid nature of small groups in Guided Math, the frequency with which a teacher meets with a group and the amount of time spent when they meet varies according to the assigned instructional tasks and needs of the group. At times, a group meeting may consist of a brief pulse-check to be sure it is on task and its members understand the mathematical concepts with which it is currently working. At other times, the group may require more intensive work with the teacher, especially if its members are struggling with new concepts or problem solving. By meeting with small groups, teachers can take into account all aspects of the instructional goals for each group to design customized plans of instruction. Teachers are able to teach at the point of need of each group, nudging their students forward along the continuum of mathematical understanding.

Mathematical communication is an integral aspect of small-group mathematics lessons. The intimacy of the small group encourages students to share their thoughts, even those students who may be reluctant to do so in a larger group. Teachers make use of this time to provide explicit systematic instruction, model the use of relevant vocabulary terms, pose thought-provoking questions to focus students' thinking, listen intently as students describe their thoughts and defend their ideas, and teach students how to carefully consider and respectfully question the thinking of their peers. The reflection required by students to verbally describe their mathematical thinking leads them to mentally organize their ideas and internalize them. The questions and comments of their peers serve to deepen and advance their conceptual understanding and mathematical agility. By listening carefully to students during these verbal exchanges and by astutely observing student work, teachers gain an invaluable insight into their students' mathematical understanding. They learn when to move ahead with instruction, when more teaching is needed, and what specific points need to be addressed for these learners—all of which help teachers as they plan future instruction to extend learning.

Close working relationships between students and the teacher or their peers in a small instructional group allows students to expand their problem-solving abilities. Vygotsky (1978) described a "zone of proximal development," the distance between the actual problem-solving ability of a learner based on what he or she can do independently and the potential ability under the guidance of an adult or with the collaboration of a peer. Fountas and Pinnell (2001) refer to it as "the learning zone." When students are supported by the teacher and by their peers, they are able to move beyond their independent capabilities. With practice, students gradually assume responsibility for these new skills. In this regard, the social nature of learning is highly supported in a small-group setting where opportunities for communication and collaboration abound.

One of the advantages of working with a small group of students as opposed to teaching a whole class is the ability to monitor student behavior more readily. With six students sitting around a small table, a teacher can easily determine when a student's attention strays, and regain it. In contrast, with a class of twenty or more, inevitably the attention of several students is not focused on the lesson. And although teachers do their best to present interesting, engaging lessons and use many methods to recapture the attention of those students, every time teachers pause to regain the attention of those students, instruction is interrupted. No matter how diligent the teacher, some students remain distracted. Working with small groups enhances the teacher's ability to maintain students' attention.

During mathematics lessons, students are often asked to complete work, practicing skills that have been taught during that lesson or a previous lesson. As students complete practice work, the teacher often circulates around the room checking their work. For those students whose work is checked at the beginning of this process, this works well. If those students have misconceptions, they are quickly identified and corrected. For students whose work is not checked until much later, this process can create difficulties. If they are working problems incorrectly, they might complete their work incorrectly before the teacher reaches them. Throughout this time, they are practicing incorrect procedures, and these misunderstandings are being reinforced through practice. When the teacher reaches them, the incorrect method has become ingrained. Correction is now much more difficult and requires greater attention from the teacher.

Teachers who are working with small groups of students, on the other hand, find it easy to monitor the work of each student. If students are making errors in their work due to misconceptions or even carelessness, the teacher notices it immediately. If the error is one that only one student is making, the misconception can be addressed by working individually with that student. If, however, the teacher notices that several students are having the same problem, work can be stopped for those students so that the teacher can reteach or clarify the concept.

An essential component of instruction is assessment. This includes formal, informal, summative, and formative assessments. To ensure student learning, often teachers engage in continuous, ongoing assessment. Much of this formative assessment occurs through the observation of students as they work and through conversations with them as they discuss their work. A correct solution is not always a valid indication of understanding. Only when students can explain their answers and the processes they used to obtain them, can teachers be assured of the students' conceptual understanding. By intently listening and observing their students and observing their interactions as they grapple with mathematical problems, teachers learn about their students and their capabilities. The small-group setting is ideal for this kind of assessment.

Challenges of Small-Group Instruction

If small-group instruction offers teachers so many advantages, why isn't all mathematics teaching done in small groups? In some cases, things simply need to be explained to the whole class. In other cases, teachers feel more comfortable teaching as they were taught. If they have never experienced working with small groups or had chances to visit other classrooms to see it in practice, planning for small groups may seem overwhelming. These teachers may wonder how to group students, how to plan instruction for small groups, and how to monitor and provide valuable, challenging work for the rest of their class as they are working with only a few students.

Small-group instruction may well require more extensive planning by teachers, as does any plan for differentiated instruction designed to address the complex needs of students. Planning for the effective use of small groups, teachers may choose to vary the content of the lesson, the way in which it is presented, or the product that students produce, while still maintaining the focus on the standards being taught. Sometimes, a common lesson is used for more than one group, but the time spent on the lesson with each group varies. Rather than planning one-size-fits-all lessons each day, teachers who use small-group instruction are involved in more complex tasks as they plan. This type of planning is only possible when teachers know their students' levels of achievement and learning needs extremely well. Teachers' wise use of ongoing, deliberate, and specific assessment, both informal and formal, gives them an understanding of their individual students and their classes. Teachers must then use this understanding to gather students together in groups, and then to provide learning opportunities that move students forward in their journeys to mathematical competency. Whether the necessity for ongoing assessment and more complex planning is a challenge perhaps depends on the perspective of the teacher. It is, however, a consideration when teachers think about using small-group instruction.

One consequence of small-group instruction is that each student receives less direct instruction from the teacher. In some classrooms, the teacher spends the entire instructional time working with the entire class. When teachers work with small groups, the remainder of the class is engaged in independent work as part of Math Workshop. Although the independent work should be meaningful, these students are working on their own. Direct teacher instruction is limited to the time when students are with the teacher in small groups. How much students learn as they work independently depends largely on the value and rigor of the tasks planned by the teacher and on how well the teacher has established procedures that allow this work to proceed uninterrupted.

So, not only must teachers plan multiple lessons for the groups with whom they will work each day, but they also have the responsibility of planning independent work, which will help students increase their mathematical understanding and which learners can complete without assistance from the teacher. Even when students are challenged with well-planned, meaningful work, for small-group instruction to function well, the actual procedures for Math Workshop must be well-planned and taught. Therefore, before implementing group work, most teachers spend a few weeks teaching the expectations for Math Workshop. In classrooms where teachers already use Guided Reading, many of these procedures overlap and may be taught at the same time.

Within the Guided Math framework, small-group instruction is a defining component, but that does not mean that it is the exclusive mode of instruction. When planning for Guided Math instruction, teachers should take into account the benefits and challenges of the teaching components so they can maximize the effectiveness and efficiency of their cumulative mathematics instruction.

Effective Uses of Small-Group Instruction

Small-group instruction is a component of Guided Math that gives teachers an enormous amount of flexibility in meeting the needs of students and gives maximum impact to their teaching. Teaching is focused precisely on the learning needs of the students in the group. Working with a small group of learners enables teachers to provide 15 to 20 minutes of "high-quality, intensive instruction that is appropriate for every member of the group" (Fountas and Pinnell 2001). The fluid nature of the group composition guarantees that students receive instruction that meets their needs. Although it is used effectively by teachers for many purposes, there are some uses for which it is particularly effective:

- differentiating instruction
- teaching mathematical "hot spots"
- teaching with manipulatives
- assessing student learning informally
- supporting mathematics process standards

Differentiating Instruction

Tomlinson (2000) describes differentiated instruction as a philosophy of teaching and learning rather than as an instructional strategy to be used when and if a teacher has time. This philosophy is based on the belief that even students who are the same age have significant differences in their readiness to learn, their interests, their styles of learning, their experiences, and their life circumstances. These differences are significant enough to impact what students need to learn, the pace at which they need to learn it, and the support they will need to learn it well.

So often however, we begin our instruction aiming toward the middle and praying for ricochet as Jennifer Taylor-Cox (2008) so aptly describes it. Then, when we discover some of our students are struggling with the concepts we are teaching, we focus our attention on their needs with the ultimate goal of boosting each and every one of our students over the bar of conceptual understanding. In the world of high-stakes testing, this focus is understandable and even laudable. Without a doubt, no child should ever be left behind.

With instruction targeting students who require the most support, middle- and high-achieving students too often languish. Typically, these students are given additional practice of skills already mastered, are asked to peer tutor other students, or are encouraged to spend time reading when they complete their assignments, rather than being moved forward with more challenging mathematical concepts. For years, teachers have been advised to provide enrichment for high-achieving students, but were strongly discouraged from allowing them to accelerate their learning. The National Mathematics Advisory Panel (2008) found, however, that gifted students benefit from having opportunities to move ahead in their mathematical learning and urged that they be permitted to do so.

In schools everywhere, teachers, individually or in professional learning groups, are reflecting on their current teaching practices and developing ways in which they can more effectively meet the learning needs of all their students—without neglecting the needs of any students. Targeting specific learning areas in small groups allows teachers to avoid the frustration inherent in the exclusive use of whole-class instruction. It allows the core of what students learn to remain constant while varying the "how" (Tomlinson 2000).

Teaching Mathematical "Hot Spots"

Most teachers, when considering the mathematics curriculum that they teach throughout the year, can identify those concepts with which their students struggle year after year. From classroom experience, they have seen how their students just don't understand some concepts in spite of well-planned lessons and, many times, in spite of the best efforts of the students themselves. These "hot spots" of instruction occur in the curriculum of every grade level. For second grade, a "hot spot" is addition and subtraction with regrouping. In fourth and fifth grades, students struggle with developing a strong conceptual understanding of fractions. In secondary classrooms, students struggle with developing a strong conceptual understanding of negative numbers.

What teacher has not, at times, longed for a smaller class so that he or she could help students grapple with these difficult concepts more effectively? Moreover, what teacher has not experienced the frustration of having a few students quickly grasp these concepts and then not having the time to move them ahead because he or she is committed to supporting those who "don't get it"?

When "hot spot" concepts are introduced, teachers that use small groups are able to closely monitor the understanding of each student in the group. Students who may be reluctant to speak up in a large group are comfortable sharing their questions. Teacher questioning provides an easy and accurate assessment tool of the initial understanding of students in the group. Based on student work and discourse, teachers can immediately adjust their instruction at any point during the lesson. If a student quickly demonstrates an understanding of the teaching point during the lesson, he or she can move out of the group and participate in Math Workshop activities.

Based on the knowledge they have from working so closely with their students, teachers can adjust their teaching methods as they introduce new concepts. Students who have already demonstrated strong foundations leading up to the new lessons may need only brief introductions before moving on to independent work. For other students who may come to the lessons with minimal background knowledge, the lessons may be lengthier and will initially focus more on the concrete aspects of the concepts to provide scaffolding for their learning. When students continue to struggle with concepts, additional work with the group can be planned to support their learning, ensuring that they all master the mathematical "hot spots."

Teaching with Manipulatives

Students retain knowledge and skills better when they are actively involved in the learning process. Research shows that 90 percent of what we both say and do is retained, compared to only 50 percent of what we hear and see (Thompson and Thompson 2005). To promote long-term knowledge and understanding, engaging students in hands-on learning with ample opportunities for discussion is essential. Using manipulatives regularly with students provides opportunities for active learning. When accompanied with meaningful conversation by students facilitated by teachers, conceptual understanding and long-term learning result.

Hiebert et al. (1997) list the following ways in which manipulatives can be used by students as tools for learning:

- providing a record of mathematical activity
- providing a way of communicating mathematical ideas
- providing an aid to thinking

Each of these ways supports the mathematical process standards recommended by NCTM (2000): problem solving, reasoning and proof, communication, connections, and representation. Through the use of manipulatives to make models, the process of representation, in effect, supports the remaining process standards. The act of creating concrete representations of mathematical concepts establishes an image of that knowledge in students' minds (Marzano, Pickering, and Pollock 2001). When students visualize and then manipulate aspects of the mathematical ideas they are exploring, they gain deeper understanding of the concept (Ennis and Witeck 2007).

As tools, however, manipulatives are only effective when students have an understanding of what they represent. For learners to use tools in ways that lead to increased understanding, they must construct meaning for the manipulatives by examining them closely, trying them out in different contexts, and listening to the ideas of others. The symbolic meaning that may seem obvious to adults is often lacking for students and is created as students have opportunities to actively use these tools following modeling and think-alouds by teachers.

Once students begin to understand the manipulatives themselves, they become a "testing ground for emerging ideas," giving learners something to ponder, explore, discuss, and use to model their mathematical ideas (Van de Walle and Lovin 2006). Even then, teachers must be aware that when students use these tools, they continue to refine their understanding of the actual tools themselves at the same time they are using them to understand other concepts.

Creating an environment where manipulatives are used effectively to build understanding is a challenge for teachers. Most elementary classrooms have collections of manipulatives available. Textbook companies recognize the effectiveness of teaching with manipulatives and frequently provide individual student sets of manipulatives as a resource to accompany their textbooks. If manipulatives are not provided through a textbook company, school systems often provide these resources for students and teachers. How often and how effectively they are used varies considerably from teacher to teacher. Often, teachers who are reluctant to make use of these resources are unsure of the classroom management techniques needed to support the effective use of the resources.

With whole-class instruction, the management of manipulatives tends to be daunting. Because instructional time is so precious, many teachers view the time spent distributing manipulatives to students as wasted time. Once they are in the students' hands, monitoring the manipulatives' use can also be frustrating. If students fail to understand the meaning of the manipulatives or how they can use them to solve problems and extend their mathematical understanding, then manipulatives are nothing more than toys. If teachers are required to interrupt instruction repeatedly to ensure manipulatives are being used productively, instructional time is lost once again. Taking these problems into consideration, it is understandable why whole-class instruction can make the daily use of manipulatives by students a challenge.

When teachers work with small groups, however, many of these hindrances are eliminated. For a start, fewer manipulatives are needed. The teacher has the manipulatives ready for use at the table where small groups meet regularly. Teachers can easily monitor the attention of students as they model the appropriate use of manipulatives and help students understand what these tools mean or represent in problem-solving situations. Students in small groups are not only more focused because of the close monitoring by the teacher, but also because they can closely watch the manipulatives being modeled by the teacher. As the responsibility for working with hands-on materials is gradually released to the students, it is easy for the teacher to interact with students. The teacher can refine or extend students' individual understanding and encourage mathematical conversations so that students can learn from each other as they examine mathematical problems, explore methods of solution, and identify questions that arise during this process.

As teachers provide meaningful and productive small-group work with manipulatives, there are several instructional rules of thumb suggested by Van de Walle and Lovin (2006).

1. Introduce new models by showing how they can represent the ideas for which they are intended.

2. Allow students (in most instances) to select freely from available models to use in solving problems.

3. Encourage the use of models when you believe it would be helpful to students having difficulty.

Working with students in small groups, as they create models using manipulatives, makes it easier for teachers to adhere to these guidelines.

Van de Walle and Lovin warn that the most widespread error that teachers make in using manipulatives is designing lessons where students are given the exact directions for using particular manipulatives to get answers to problems. Although manipulative materials are being used by students in these lessons, this practice encourages rote learning as students blindly follow set procedures. Assessing student conceptual understanding is impossible in lessons of this kind. Unfortunately, when whole-class instruction is the norm, teachers tend to resort to cookie-cutter lessons in which little individualization is encouraged. To get through the lesson quickly with a large group, it seems easier to use only one material for modeling and to clearly lay out the problem-solving steps students must follow. Teachers may erroneously believe that students who follow their directions to determine answers actually understand the mathematical concepts and then are frustrated when their students are unable to transfer this rote learning to other situations.

Meeting with students in small groups lets teachers give students more flexibility in choosing the manipulatives to use and in trying alternative methods of problem solving. A variety of materials is easily organized and made available to students as the students explore various strategies for problem solving. Teachers are able to closely observe the students' attempts at model making and problem solving. Later, as students share their problem-solving successes and mistakes, the entire group benefits from the experiences of its individuals.

Formative Assessment: Assessment For Learning

Assessment is a critical element of effective teaching. Only when we know what we want our students to learn and where they are on the learning curve can we plan instruction that truly meets their needs. Of course, knowing where they are cognitively isn't always easy since where they are changes constantly.

When teachers rely primarily on end-of-unit tests to evaluate the learning of their students, they are not taking advantage of opportunities to monitor progress. Additionally, they either make the assumption that all students are learning exactly what is being taught, or they think that whether their students learn is not really their responsibility. If they have "taught" it, they have done their jobs. After the test, they will see if the students have done theirs.

This is a rather harsh view of teachers. Fortunately, most teachers are deeply committed to student learning and feel a much greater responsibility to their students than this description implies. With the increased emphasis on accountability as a result of high-stakes testing, teachers face even greater pressure to ensure student success. In addition to chapter tests, teachers monitor daily work and homework assignments. They give quizzes and assign projects. All of these are examples of formative assessments that provide evidence of student learning. Although the information gained from these assessments is timelier than that from unit tests, there are still time gaps between the actual instruction and the assessment data.

Ideally, to plan and deliver instruction effectively, teachers continuously monitor student performance for evidence of learning and to identify specific learning needs. What they learn about their students from this ongoing assessment allows them to adjust their instruction "on the run." Ongoing informal assessment is a formative assessment, or assessment *for* learning, as opposed to summative assessment, or assessment *of* learning, because it lets teachers respond to learning needs as and when needed.

An additional distinction of formative assessment is the involvement of students in setting achievement goals and in the assessment process itself. Since assessments for learning focus on the day-to-day progress of students toward meeting their goals, teachers are able to provide timely descriptive feedback to let students know precisely where they are in relation to where they need to be academically and exactly what they need to do to reach their goals (Stiggins 2005). These are powerful ways to help focus student learning. Linking assessment and learning not only results in students becoming more aware of the "how" of learning, but also leads to more student ownership and investment in learning (Davies 2000). In small-group instruction, teachers have the ability to interact closely with their students so that assessment of this kind is possible. With experience, the process of teaching and assessing informally becomes interwoven, one affecting the other, leading to a flexible, but durable fabric of instruction.

Supporting Mathematics Process Standards

The discipline of mathematics is complex. To become effective mathematicians, students need to master a myriad of skills and develop a deep conceptual understanding of crucial mathematical content. Teachers focus on helping students understand numbers and operations, algebra, measurement, geometry, and data analysis and probability—the content areas outlined in the National Council of Teachers of Mathematics standards (2000).

The content standards are only a part of the Principles and Standards for School Mathematics established by the NCTM. The remaining standards address the processes mathematicians use. To achieve competency in mathematics, students must also learn to problem solve, offer mathematical reasoning and proof for their mathematical ideas, communicate mathematically, make mathematical connections, and represent mathematical ideas accurately. These process standards are an integral part of the discipline, and ones which have often been neglected as procedural competency, demonstrated through computation, was stressed. In fact, for some people, mathematical skills and computation are synonymous. Frequently, the mathematical questions on high-stakes testing confirm that assumption.

In recent years, concerns have grown about the mathematical competency of our students as comparisons of their performances to those of young people in other countries have been conducted. Students from the United States no longer rank near the top in these comparisons. As educators have begun to examine exemplary mathematical instructional practices, it has become apparent that the process skills outlined by the NCTM are a critical component of mathematics education. It is crucial that students be provided with opportunities to cultivate both content and process skills to ensure that they develop deep conceptual understanding and the ability to apply their mathematical knowledge.

In spite of the strong connection between the content and process standards, the process standards are often bypassed as teachers struggle to cover the content required by state curriculum standards. Additionally, because teachers tend to teach the same ways in which they were taught, many are unsure how these standards should be taught. Teachers are searching for effective ways to integrate the process skills into their lessons.

The kinds of learning experiences educators provide clearly determine the development of mathematical understanding in students. Students who are actively engaged in well-chosen problem-solving tasks accompanied by focused discourse begin to grasp the process standards as they hone their procedural fluency. Because many instances where content and process learning build on each other are not simple worksheet assignments, teachers often find it difficult to execute them in a whole-class setting.

Working with small groups of students with similar learning needs allows teachers the flexibility that they need to address the process skills in their instruction. The teacher can challenge students to solve problems while offering support through carefully crafted questions. Students in these groups are encouraged to discuss their mathematical efforts as they work together—to question, to reason, and to reflect. Manipulatives are easily managed with students as they create models to represent their mathematical ideas. As students share the strategies they are using, teachers help them translate their ideas into mathematically appropriate vocabulary and then guide them as they extend their understanding.

Teachers who are searching for ways to incorporate more complex learning activities and tasks into their instructional plans often find that they are able to try in small groups what they would be hesitant to attempt with the whole class. With these initial trials, teachers discover that student interest and excitement about mathematics increase, along with student motivation.

Forming Small Groups for Learning

In any classroom, one finds students with wide ranges of experience, background knowledge, and skills. Additionally, once the students enter the classroom, they will progress at varying rates (Fountas and Pinnell 1996). So, some grouping for instructional purposes makes sense.

In the past, instructional groupings of children were based on data from lagging indicators including grades, standardized tests from the previous year, and even recommendations from past teachers. Only the general ability of students was considered. Once placed in a group at the beginning of the school year, a student remained in that group. And, consequently, since instruction was based on progressing through a set sequence of materials, there was not much opportunity for students to catch up with higher groups. More than likely, they remained in the same groups year after year. Students in higher groups who might have difficulty with a particular concept were moved along at the same pace and with the same instruction as those students who mastered it quickly. If they didn't get it, so be it—maybe they would next year. Conversely, students in the lower groups who quickly mastered some areas of the curriculum were still forced to go through additional instruction until the other students mastered it or until it was time to move on.

Too frequently in the past, minority students and students from economically disadvantaged homes were assigned to the low groups. The rigidity of traditional grouping guaranteed that these children would remain there. Students in these groups were often the ones who were inundated with worksheets in misguided attempts to help them catch up while the higher groups were allowed to explore mathematical concepts and learn through mathematical games. Falling further behind, too many of these students lost confidence in their mathematical abilities, ceased trying to succeed, and in some cases, dropped out of school as soon as they could.

Grouping in Guided Math differs from the previously discussed grouping model. It proposes flexible, needs-based instructional grouping that changes to accommodate the learning needs of budding mathematicians. The composition of these groups also may vary from concept to concept. In fact, one of the aspects of Guided Math with which teachers struggle is determining exactly how students should be grouped to most effectively and efficiently meet students' needs.

Forming Guided Reading groups is a more clear-cut process than forming Guided Math groups. Teachers assess reading levels by performing running records as their students read aloud. This formative assessment lets the teacher know the reading level of each student. For regular Guided Reading lessons, those levels determine grouping. At any time, as a teacher observes changes in reading levels, students may move from one group to another. In addition, groups may be formed for specific needs, as they are identified.

For mathematics, there is no one assessment that can help teachers determine mathematical readiness levels. Furthermore, there is no mathematics leveling system that corresponds to the multiple reading leveling systems available to teachers. Although there are overarching concepts in mathematics, from domain to domain, the capability of a student may vary. So, how are teachers to determine similar mathematical needs for student grouping?

Because Guided Math is a framework that is adapted by teachers to meet the instructional needs in their classrooms, there is not one correct way to determine student groups. Teachers usually find that a combination of assessment methods work best for them. These assessments include unit pre-tests, looking at evidence of learning from previous sequential concepts, formative tests, proficiency levels in relevant performance tasks, observations of students as they work, conversations with students, and benchmark tests.

Unit Pre-tests

Some teachers prefer to give an initial assessment at the beginning of a unit to help them discover the areas of strengths and needs of their students. It is essential that the pre-test be closely aligned with the curricular standards that students will learn during the unit. Teachers then examine the data to form groups of students with similar needs for the coming unit, keeping in mind that as the unit progresses, the composition of the groups will change.

Performance with Previous Sequential Concepts

At times, a new unit will consist of concepts that build directly on those taught in an earlier unit. For example, in some second grade classes, a study of place value precedes a unit on addition or subtraction with regrouping. Students who do not completely understand place value are likely to need more support with the unit on addition or subtraction with regrouping than students who have demonstrated a strong understanding of place value. In these circumstances, teachers may be able to form groups without pre-testing their students.

Formative Tests

As students work through a unit of study, many teachers administer brief paper-and-pencil formative tests to help them identify how their students are doing with the new concepts. Since Guided Math group composition is fluid, groups may be adjusted to reflect the instructional needs of individual students based on the findings from the assessments. To be effective, these assessments are administered throughout the unit rather than waiting until teachers feel that most students have mastered the concepts being taught. By assessing often during the unit and then immediately using their results, teachers target the unique needs of their students, providing additional support or additional challenges.

Performance Tasks

Performance standards comprise the curriculum in an ever-increasing number of states. Just as the moniker implies, students are expected to demonstrate their competence by being able to perform specified tasks. Instructional units based on performance standards now include a variety of tasks for students. Students are provided rubrics that specify exactly what teachers expect to find in exemplary work. As teachers teach their students to use rubrics to assess and then revise their work, the knowledge that teachers gain helps them identify the next steps in learning for their students. By grouping together students who have the same next steps, teachers are able to efficiently meet their students' needs and maximize learning.

Observations of Student Work

Many teachers know that assessment is an ongoing process; it is more than testing and performance tasks. They know that the sooner they are able to detect misunderstanding, the easier it is to correct. The sooner they find students have grasped a new concept, the sooner they can move them on to the next teaching point. By observing students as they work, teachers can fine-tune and focus their instruction. To manage information from observations, some teachers use checklists, others simply record anecdotal notes. Teachers develop recording systems based on their own preferences, but the importance of recording these observations can't be overstated. Although it's tempting to think that one will be able to remember what has been observed, more likely than not, all but the most obvious observations are forgotten as the day progresses. Recording observations as they occur provides an accurate overview of student learning and needs. Based on these observations, teachers can plan to have Guided Math groups meet just once to address a misconception or meet for a more extended period to reinforce learning of difficult concepts.

Mathematical Conversations with Students

Just as experienced teachers recognize the wisdom of observing students as they work, they know the value of engaging students in conversation about their work and their mathematical understanding. Just because a student came up with the correct answer doesn't necessarily mean he or she understands the concepts involved. When a teacher is able to listen to learners explain what they did to arrive at an answer or explain why they think a conjecture is or is not true, the degree of conceptual understanding of the student becomes crystal clear. Once again, arriving at an efficient recording system is essential. It is virtually impossible to retain an accurate mental record of what has been gleaned from student conversations. With these observations recorded, teachers are able to plan groupings to address the needs of their students.

Benchmark Tests

Some school districts are creating benchmark tests to determine student progress toward meeting either the grading-period learning goals or year-end learning goals. The data from these assessments is certainly more current than that from the state standardized tests from the previous year, yet it comes a little too late to use effectively in grouping students for daily instruction. Despite these limitations, the data does allow teachers to identify students who appear to still have some gaps in their learning. A teacher would be remiss if he or she failed to use this information to address those gaps. By grouping students according to the documented gaps and addressing the areas of need until students demonstrate their understanding, teachers can ensure that their learners truly master the curriculum goals.

Organizing for Small-Group Instruction

An essential element in effective small-group instruction is a well-organized work area. Teachers with limited teaching time want to make the most of it. When the meeting space is clearly defined and any materials needed are prepared and readily available at the beginning of each math class, group instruction can begin promptly. Even good teachers with excellent lessons can squander valuable time if they have to clear off the tables to be used, gather the resources needed, and remind students to return to their desks for pencils or paper during the time scheduled for small-group instruction. Giving thought to organizational details as lessons are planned, leads to efficient use of this precious instructional time.

Most often teachers meeting with small groups choose to use small tables that will accommodate up to six students and the teacher. In some classrooms, teachers choose to meet with students on carpeted areas of the floor or at groupings of desks. The choice of meeting space is up to the teacher, but it should be carefully considered and designated before small-group instruction is begun in a classroom. The location of these work areas should also allow teachers clear views of students who are working independently so that their activities can be monitored. If a co-teacher is in the room during mathematics instruction, the classroom teacher may consider establishing a second area where students can meet to work in small groups. Whatever areas teachers designate for work with small groups, they should be uncluttered and ready for use as mathematics class begins daily.

The small group is meeting on the floor instead of at a table.

These designated areas should be equipped with the materials teachers and students most often use as they explore mathematical concepts and problems solving. Although students may have the supplies at their desks, the goal is to maximize the instructional time for each group. Even responsible students have been known to forget to bring needed materials to work areas. If the materials are already there for student use, time is not wasted while students return to their desks or try to find other students from whom they can borrow pencils. The following are suggested items to have available during small-group instruction:

- whiteboard(s)
- chart pad and easel
- work mats
- manipulatives
- measuring tools
- paper
- pencils
- erasers
- crayons
- markers
- specific materials for the lesson planned

In order to address individual students' needs, it helps teachers when they have ready access to student assessment data at hand—both formal and perhaps more importantly, the informal. As teachers work with individual students, they can refer back to anecdotal notes from earlier observations, citing both the student's strengths and the next learning steps needed. Along with the previously recorded data, teachers should keep at hand materials to record their observations of current student work. These materials may include checklists that show evidence of students' learning or simply organized systems to record dated notes about what students can do and understand with additional notations about which areas they need more work.

When teachers use small-group instruction during their mathematics classes, it is obvious that some time must be spent in student transitions from one activity to another. To make transitions go smoothly, effective teachers plan exactly how students can most efficiently move from one learning activity to another with as little disruption as possible. Once visions of how that should occur are in place, they can break them down into teachable components so that students can understand precisely how the visions work and then actually take the steps necessary to realize them. Students need to know not only the procedures they will follow to make the transitions, but they also have to be able to follow them—that takes practice. At the beginning of the school year, teachers can work with their students for a week or two, having students repeatedly practice the procedures before they begin to work with small groups. Throughout the school year, at times, teachers can revisit these procedures with their students to ensure swift, orderly transitions.

Guided Math Lessons for Small Groups

Before beginning a small-group lesson, it is important to plan instruction and get organized (Figure 5.1). Even though only a portion of the class is participating, the same level of preparedness is required as if you were creating a lesson for the entire class.

Figure 5.1 Planning Guided Math Lessons for Small Groups

Planning the Lesson
1. Determine the big ideas of the unit of study to be taught based on the standards and the needs of the students.
2. Decide what the criteria of success will be in mastering the standards in the unit.
3. Use information from assessments (both formal and informal) to form groups based on student needs.
4. Select specific teaching points for each group.
5. Prepare differentiated lessons based on the learning needs of the students in each group.
6. Gather and organize the materials necessary for the lesson.

Identify the Big Ideas

Having established the procedures for working with small groups, the next step is planning the instruction, taking into consideration the standards to be mastered and the needs of the students. Within every unit of study, there are "big ideas" that are essential to the conceptual understanding of the standards within the unit. These are the central organizing ideas of mathematics principles (Fosnot and Dolk 2001). Students not only need to learn the big ideas of mathematics—they also need to learn the mathematical way of thinking. They need to know how these ideas were generated by mathematicians (Van de Walle and Lovin 2006). These ideas are the basic concepts that students should understand and be able to apply appropriately. These enduring conceptual understandings comprise the foundation for mathematical growth. They entail more than simply learning set procedures and developing automaticity with math facts.

Establish Criteria for Success

Keeping these conceptual big ideas in mind, teachers often collaborate to decide exactly what students need to be able to do to master the standards of the unit of study. In schools where collaboration is not the norm, individual teachers have the responsibility of determining the criteria for success for their students. Exactly what are the expectations for student work? What will be considered evidence of student success? How does a student demonstrate proficiency? Whether the criteria is a result of collaboration or is established by individual teachers, it is the basis for assessing the learning of students and as such, guides the planning of instruction. The criteria may be based upon performance tasks, observational checklists, or written tests.

Use Data to Form Groups

Maintaining a focus on the big ideas, the standards, and the criteria for success, teachers turn to the data they have gathered from a variety of assessment sources to form small groups of students with similar needs. A group may meet together for only one lesson or may meet throughout the entire unit of study. The flexibility of the group composition ensures that each student's instruction matches his or her needs. Students should work just beyond their independent capability, but within the area where they can be successful with support from a teacher or peers. Working within Vygotsky's (1978) zone of proximal development, learning is maximized. Students who work beyond the group to which they are assigned may be moved. If a student begins to flounder in a given group, he or she may be moved to a group that better addresses his or her current needs.

Teachers can use the same considerations to determine how frequently they should meet with their groups. When creating a schedule for small-group instruction, flexibility is still the key. Lower-achieving students require more supported instruction and should be met with as frequently as possible. Higher-achieving students may meet with the teacher briefly and then work independently.

Although small-group instruction with these students may occur less often and be of shorter duration, it is, nevertheless, important. In these instructional sessions, teachers help these learners refine and extend their conceptual understanding. Traditionally, the needs of higher-achieving students have been neglected as those of struggling learners demand the instructional time of teachers. Within the Guided Math framework, teachers are also able to target the learning needs of the higher-achieving students.

It helps to have a weekly schedule of when each group will meet during the week. In the example shown below (Figure 5.2), Group 1 is really struggling with the standards being addressed, so the teacher will meet with them four times during this week. Group 2 has a better grasp of the concepts being taught, but still needs considerable support. They will meet on Monday, Tuesday, and Wednesday. Since Group 3 is doing pretty well, it will only meet twice during the week. Group 4 has demonstrated mastery of the unit standards, so the teacher is extending their learning. They will meet on Friday to receive instruction extending the grade-level curriculum. The following week, they will work on tasks aligned to this instruction. To manage the instructional time, the teacher only meets with two groups per day. Depending on the allotted instructional time and the needs of students, it may be possible to meet with more than two groups per day.

Figure 5.2 Weekly Schedule for Math Groups

Group	Mon.	Tues.	Wed.	Thu.	Fri.
1. Felisa, Nori, Brad, Ray, Davisha	x	x	x	x	
2. Ricardo, Marcus, Karina, Tameshia, Portia	x	x	x		
3. Dimitri, Tonya, Mary Beth, Carlos, Keon				x	x
4. Min, Monica, Quin, Lucas, Rosa					x

This is only an example of how small-group instruction may be scheduled. Teachers should take into account their individual classes when planning. The schedule may vary from week to week. With this particular schedule, groups meet on consecutive days. That often works well to provide continuity for the lessons. This allows lessons to extend over several days without a gap between them. Some teachers prefer to spread the lessons out throughout the week instead of grouping them this way.

Another element to consider is the behavior of students in the groups. With this weekly schedule, both Group 1 and Group 2 are working independently on Friday. If these groups have built up the endurance necessary to work independently for the entire class period, this schedule will work. However, if the students in these two groups cannot behave appropriately for that length of independent time, the teacher may prefer to only have one of these groups working independently for the whole class period on any given day. The planning of small-group instruction allows teachers to create a plan that best fits the needs of their classes. It may take a few tries and adjustments before a teacher arrives at a good schedule. Even then, it may need adjustments during the year.

Determine Teaching Points

How do teachers determine what the next learning steps are for their small groups? An easy answer is to refer back to the data used to form the groups. Since groups are established based on common needs, those needs provide an instructional compass for teachers. This is in contrast to the traditional grouping of students where they were grouped together in high, middle, and low groups. Without specific data by which they could navigate, teachers often blindly followed the sequence of the instructional materials they were given without varying their instruction to meet the specific learning needs of their students.

Teachers today are fortunate to have an array of student data available to guide them as they make these important instructional decisions. The data is only a benefit to teachers, however, when it targets the relevant curriculum areas, is available in a timely manner, and is used effectively by teachers. Looking at lagging indicators of student success, such as grades from the previous year or standardized state assessments, generally supplies only broad overviews of the achievement levels of individual students. The data is too broad and is certainly not timely. Teachers can use this data to identify overall needs and trends, but not to determine daily, targeted lessons.

The data from formative assessments allows teachers to examine student achievement on specific standards and elements. For example, according to NCTM standards (2000), all students in grades 3–5 should "recognize and generate equivalent forms of commonly used fractions, decimals, and percents." Let's say that a student named Nina demonstrates that she can recognize equivalent fractions. Her teacher has observed her working with a variety of representations successfully. In addition, her verbal explanation of her work indicates that she has a clear understanding of this portion of the standard. It would be a disservice to Nina to place her in a group in which the students were still struggling with that concept.

Later, when Nina was given a brief written formative assessment, she had trouble generating equivalent fractions. Clearly, she needs some extra instructional support to meet that part of the standard. Nina's learning would be best supported by her inclusion in a group of students who share her individual needs. A teacher planning instruction for this group would have no difficulty identifying an appropriate teaching point based on the data from these formative assessments.

Nina's next step in meeting this standard would be to learn how to generate equivalent fractions, not just recognize them. The teacher, in planning instruction, would want to challenge the group with work that was just beyond what they are capable of doing independently. With teacher scaffolding to boost conceptual understanding, students stretch to achieve greater proficiency. The laser sharp accuracy of this kind of instruction efficiently keeps students on track in their learning, with no instructional gaps or unnecessary repetitions of instruction.

To identify the next steps in learning for students in small groups, teachers need to look first at the curriculum standards and then use the data from a variety of formative assessments, both informal and formal. Using this data, teachers can try to identify the highest level of understanding with which the group of students has achieved proficiency and can then move to the next sequential or logical teaching point. Throughout this teaching process, the composition of the groups changes as student needs change. Some students are going to have an "aha" moment when a concept suddenly makes sense to them, while the rest of the group is still working on understanding. That student should be moved to a group whose needs more closely align with his or hers. Conversely, while the rest of the group has mastered a standard, one or two students may still struggle. The struggling students' needs are better served in a group that is continuing to work on that standard. Teacher instruction always varies to support students as they work in their groups and move toward mathematical understanding and proficiency.

Prepare Differentiated Lessons

To support students' learning, teachers use the data they have collected when deciding what to do to help their students take the next steps in their mathematical development. Identifying appropriate teaching points helps teachers begin the process of differentiating instruction for each group. Not only does the frequency and length of time vary for each group, but the content of the lesson and the level of support provided are differentiated based on student needs.

The intent of the teacher when planning the instruction is to present a lesson that is at the right level of difficulty for the learners in the group. If a lesson is too easy, the students will breeze through it with very little thought. Some students, when bored, try to avoid the work completely or else they become behavior problems. Whatever the reaction of the students when presented with work that demands little of them, it is unproductive for learning.

When the lesson is too difficult, on the other hand, students become discouraged and frustrated. All of us have at one time or another been in situations where we were in over our heads. From experience, we know that feeling as if we are drowning is not conducive to learning. In these situations, as with lessons that are too easy, students tend to shut down cognitively. Some may thoughtlessly go through a series of procedures that they have been "taught" and hope for the best. Others feel a strong sense of inadequacy as they attempt this work and develop negative attitudes toward mathematics that may last whole lifetimes.

The small-group environment is a perfect place for students to stretch their mathematical wings. Students learn best when they feel supported and free to take risks. When this environment is coupled with mathematical challenges taking students beyond their current understanding, students' mathematical understanding flourishes. Effective teachers refuse to spoon-feed their learners, but instead allow them to grapple with problems so that they can finally feel the satisfaction of independently completing difficult tasks. All the while, however, these teachers are guiding their students' work with thoughtful questions and helping them discover strategies that will lead them to success. As students struggle to discover effective problem-solving strategies and make mathematical sense of their world, and as they become puzzled and intrigued by mathematical questions they face, they "begin the real journey of doing and constructing mathematics" (Fosnot and Dolk 2001). The increased proficiency and conceptual understanding these students develop provides a solid foundation for middle school and high school. By setting up learning situations where students work at just the right levels, teachers gently prod their students to reach their full potentials.

Differentiation can also be based on the teachers' knowledge of the learning styles of their students. Generally, presenting information in a variety of ways benefits all students. For auditory learners, songs or chants reinforce concepts. Tactile and kinesthetic learners benefit from hands-on activities where manipulatives are used for modeling or activities that match up numerical concepts with specific hand or body motions. Visual learners do well when concepts are represented in graphic organizers. And, as beneficial as it may be to support specific learning styles, it benefits learners to participate in activities that employ learning styles other than those in which they are strongest. By using learning styles other than those which come naturally to them, students become stronger, more agile learners. When students are given opportunities to learn mathematical concepts through multiple learning strategies, they are more likely to acquire comprehensive conceptual understandings, which allow them to flexibly manipulate mathematical ideas and apply them in new contexts.

Gather Materials

Once the lesson has been conceived, the teacher should gather together the necessary materials. It is important to anticipate everything that may be needed for the instruction. Even the best lessons can be rendered ineffective for the lack of materials. Lack of time or poor organization sometimes leads to teachers being unprepared and having to improvise as they teach. Although this will certainly happen to every teacher at times during their teaching careers, it should only occur rarely. For effective use of the limited time available for small-group instruction, priority should be given to preparation. Even when the use of manipulatives is not a part of the planned lesson, students may have trouble with abstract aspects of the instruction and require them. If teachers anticipate the supports students may need and have those materials within easy reach, the lesson is uninterrupted.

Teaching a Guided Math Lesson with a Small Group

The procedures for a small-group lesson are very similar to that of a whole-group lesson. The steps in Figure 5.3 detail how to teach a Guided Math lesson with a small group.

Figure 5.3 Teaching a Guided Math Lesson with a Small Group

Guided Math in a Small Group

1. Briefly introduce the lesson by providing supportive strategies for learners through a mini lesson to introduce or extend the concepts being learned.

2. Provide students with a clear understanding of the activity or task on which they will work, including setting criteria for success.

3. Encourage students to use a variety of strategies to solve the problem or complete the activity.

4. Scaffold student learning by giving just enough support to move students to the next level of understanding and proficiency.

5. Provide ample opportunities for mathematical discourse.

6. Give students specific, descriptive feedback on their work and encourage students to engage in self-assessment based on the criteria for success.

Introduce the Lesson

A small-group lesson should focus on a specific aspect of a larger concept with student activities that challenge, yet can be mastered with scaffolded support. As the lesson begins, teachers should introduce the problems or activities of the lesson by providing supporting strategies that will help students refine or extend their present mathematical understanding. This can be accomplished through a brief mini lesson or a demonstration with a think-aloud. The emphasis is on *brief* because students should be directly engaged with mathematics during most of small-group instruction. The goal of this instruction is to extend the independent mathematical skills of students. During the introduction of the lesson, teachers may:

- Help students connect mathematical concepts to their own lives, to their knowledge of the world, to another aspect of mathematics, or to a similar problem they have solved.

- Demonstrate the kinds of questions mathematicians may ask about problems as they work on solving them.

- Encourage students to reflect on mathematical concepts they have already mastered.

- Teach students how to visualize problems as a first step toward solving them.

- Focus on mathematical vocabulary terms or other vocabulary terms in word problems that may be difficult for students.

- Support students in their efforts to pick out important ideas in mathematical concepts and important details in math problems.

- Demonstrate how to use manipulatives.

- Emphasize the importance of students monitoring their own work by checking for errors, revisiting the criteria for success, and thinking about whether their work makes sense.

- Encourage the use of multiple representations of mathematical ideas as a way to communicate ideas, solve problems, and interpret mathematical phenomena.

Present the Activity or Task

Following the mini lesson, the teacher should provide clear directions to the students, describing the activity they will complete or the task to be performed. If written materials are provided, it is important to know that each student in the group understands what is expected. Students should begin work with knowledge of what constitutes success with the given assignment. Teachers may provide rubrics or checklists that detail expectations, or they may show students exemplars of work on similar activities. As instruction moves away from almost exclusively using paper-and-pencil computation assessments, teachers have the responsibility of letting students know what they expect students to achieve and how students will be assessed. By giving students this knowledge before they begin work, they have opportunities to monitor their own progress as they work. The more teachers can stimulate students to monitor their thinking and their work, the better their mathematical work will be (Hyde 2006).

Encourage the Use of Multiple Strategies

Traditionally, word problems appear at the end of worksheets. Students are asked to solve them almost as an afterthought and perhaps with little instructional support. The problems are connected to the concepts covered in the rest of the worksheet, but are typically very contrived and not connected to real life. Students often plug in whatever procedures they used for the rest of the page without giving the problems much thought.

As new mathematics standards are being introduced across the country, teachers' understandings of mathematics instruction are expanding. More often now, students encounter more problem-solving challenges and tasks that not only relate to their lives, but also involve multiple areas of mathematics. Standards have also helped teachers see that performing simple procedures demonstrates low levels of mathematical achievement. Students must have much deeper conceptual understandings of mathematics. One way in which students develop these understandings is by learning that there are almost always multiple strategies that can be used to solve problems.

During small-group instruction, students should be encouraged to choose which strategy they should use, drawing upon strategies that have already been introduced or by using what they know to create new strategies. When they are able to do this, they demonstrate deep conceptual understandings. If teachers prescribe the one "correct" way to solve a problem, students soon stop relying on their own reasoning and stop thinking, especially when they think they've forgotten the "correct" procedure for solving a particular type of problem. Standard algorithms for problem solving become abstract recipes for answers that must be memorized, but have no meaning.

If, instead, students listen to their teacher's explanations while problem solving, see multiple strategies used by their peers, and experiment with strategies themselves, they develop abilities to generalize about mathematical principles (Hyde 2006). Eventually, as they continue to work with mathematical tasks, they can mentally envision models and representations of mathematical concepts and move beyond concrete and symbolic to more abstract mathematical knowledge.

Scaffold Learning

Students working in small-group instruction are supported in their learning with carefully considered scaffolding by teachers. Scaffolding originally referred to the way parents interact with their children as they learn. As children begin to learn something new, they are highly supported by their parents. In these learning situations, children supported in tasks they cannot do independently, but only with the assistance of an adult or more capable peer are working in what was described by Vygotsky as the zone of proximal development (1978). This adult support is gradually withdrawn as the child becomes more independent. The learning process can be viewed as a joint social achievement involving both the child and the parents. Parents are constantly monitoring and responding to their children's increased proficiency by gradually releasing responsibility for the task. The role of teachers as they scaffold learning is similar to that of the parent, but focused more on explicit learning in a group setting rather than in a one-on-one environment (Myhill, Jones, and Hopper 2006).

The use of scaffolding is highly effective in extending the learning of students. According to Owocki (2003) and Myhill et al. (2006), for teacher support and interaction to be true scaffolding, it must have the following characteristics:

- Scaffolding occurs with assistance. One or more students engage collaboratively with a teacher or another student to acquire new knowledge, skills, or understanding. Learning is a social process.

- Scaffolding involves inter-subjectivity. The participants in the learning activity strive for a common view and adjust to the perspectives and needs of each other—just as with a child and parent.

- Scaffolding is provided with warmth and a responsiveness toward students' needs. The teacher warmly provides just enough support to help the learners be successful while still allowing students to develop a deeper conceptual understanding. Rather than the teacher's role being that of dispenser of knowledge, it is that of a caring supporter in the learner's quest for knowledge.

- Scaffolding is focused. Instructional support focuses on a particular skill or aspect of understanding. This helps the student concentrate on mastering one particular aspect of a more global concept.

- Scaffolding avoids failure. The instructional tasks are designed to be challenging to the students, yet achievable.

- Scaffolding is temporary. As teachers consider ways to support learning, they also plan how to gradually, when it is appropriate, remove the support and turn responsibility over to students. Thus, scaffolding provides the temporary, yet essential, assistance many learners need to reach "the next step."

(Adapted from Owocki 2003 and Myhill et al. 2006)

It is also important to have current, reliable data of student learning, and use that data to plan and adjust instruction to scaffold the learning of the students. Teachers who understand their students' achievements and needs can accurately respond by turning over responsibility to their students in a timely manner. However, this is not an exact art. It is easy to hold on too long in fear that a student might falter. But, teachers must watch for signs that students are ready to assume more independence, and then let them spread their wings and fly.

Promote Mathematical Discourse

One of the simplest things that teachers can do to promote student understanding is to be sure they reflect on what they are doing and communicate about it to others (Hiebert et al. 1997). Learning is naturally a social process. When students work in a small group, the likelihood that they will participate in a mathematical conversation increases dramatically. There are some students who will have their say in any learning environment, but students who are shy, lack confidence, or are unsure about their mathematical ideas often refrain from sharing them. When students are silent, they are forced to make sense of what they are learning in isolation (Nichols 2006). Small-group instruction provides a more intimate setting and makes these students more comfortable. It also makes it easier for teachers to be sure that all voices are heard.

In addition to the cognitive benefit of having to reflect and organize their thoughts before they speak, students also tend to retain what they have learned longer when they have to communicate it orally or in writing. Thoughtful discussion also helps students:

- summarize and synthesize information
- make inferences and conjectures
- justify their thinking
- expand their mathematical vocabulary
- confirm and extend their understanding
- discover errors in their thinking
- develop the ability to question the ideas of others in a productive way

Students who learn to consult with others to resolve mathematical dilemmas begin to recognize that wrestling with these ideas is not just about finding answers, but is really more about growing ideas (Nichols 2006).

Teachers can also use questioning to stimulate and expand the thinking of their students. The conversational tone they use serves as a model. By following the lead of the teacher, students learn to respect the ideas of others whether they agree with them or not. When the teacher uses an error as a teachable moment rather than a failure, students begin to realize that their errors are just stepping stones in their mathematical growth.

Almost as important as having opportunities to share ideas in a group conversation about their work is being asked to write about it. Many teachers ask students to maintain Math Journals in which they record their strategies, justifications, understandings, and reflections. Journals are often also used to record applicable mathematical vocabulary—frequently with definitions in the students' own words, nonlinguistic representations, and examples and nonexamples. Before students are asked to reflect in these journals, teachers should model the kind of writing they expect to see, thinking aloud as they do so. As a next step, using shared writing, the class can create a written reflection on its math work, on chart paper, to be displayed in the classroom as a sample of how it should look. Students should have several opportunities to see what this kind of writing might look like before being asked to reflect in writing in their Math Journals.

If Math Journals are not used, teachers should at least have their students include written explanations or reflections of their work as part of their daily math assignments. Again, as with writing in Math Journals, the process should be modeled repeatedly before students are asked to do it independently.

Promote Learning by Giving Feedback

Although feedback exists in many different forms, everyone receives it during his or her daily life. Teachers receive feedback when a student exclaims, "Oh, now I get it!" Feedback is also received when class work is checked only to discover that most of the students failed to understand the lesson. Whether positive or negative, feedback provides direction.

Effective feedback lets people know exactly what needs to be done to achieve success in whatever they are working on. Simply telling a baseball player that he or she has struck out too many times doesn't improve his performance. Hitting coaches know that they need to give very specific feedback on batting stance, the speed of the swing, or how the bat is held in order to help a player improve his or her batting average. With specific descriptive feedback, the baseball player can make corrections and, through practice, improve his or her performance.

Descriptive feedback for students lets them know about their learning. It includes specific information about what students are doing well and what they are not doing well (Davies 2000). In a small group of students, when the criteria for success have already been established, teachers are able to provide effective feedback to students as they work. Instead of waiting until a task is completed and then evaluating it, teachers can immediately focus students on areas in which they are not meeting the criteria so that those areas can be improved before the work is turned in to be evaluated.

Of course, students need ample feedback about what they are doing well, too. When they know exactly what they are doing well, they can replicate those things in future work. Recognizing a student's efforts also increases student motivation to continue doing those things. According to Anne Davies (2000), descriptive feedback:

- comes both during and after the learning
- is easily understood
- relates directly to the learning
- is specific, so performance can improve
- involves choice on the part of the learner as to the type of feedback and how to receive it
- is part of an ongoing conversation about the learning
- is in comparison to models, exemplars, samples, or descriptions
- is about the performance or the work—not the person

When students have been taught how to give descriptive feedback based on specific criteria, they can self-assess their work or give feedback to peers. Not only can this practice improve students' learning in the classroom, but by teaching students how to monitor their work, they are learning a skill that they can use throughout their lives.

When the lesson ends, the teacher can maximize future instruction by accurately recording observations, selecting the next steps in learning, identifying students who need additional help, and changing the group composition, if necessary (Figure 5.4).

Figure 5.4 Teacher Reflection Process after a Lesson

Teacher Reflection after the Lesson

1. Record and organize informal assessment information based on observations and conversations.

2. Select the next steps in learning for the group, as well as for individual students.

3. Identify students who are struggling with specific concepts, and plan how to reteach the concept when needed.

4. Change the composition of the groups, when appropriate.

Keep Records of Informal Assessments

When teachers are working with small groups of students, they are able to listen to student conversations, observe their work, and in general, get a feel for the levels of student understanding. If these observations are recorded, they can be referred to when planning instruction or meeting with parents. There are a variety of recording systems used by teachers to maintain the anecdotal notes they make during their work with the group.

Here are a few suggestions for keeping records:

- Create a spiral notebook that has a section for each student and mark the pages by divider tabs. During instruction, open to the section for a student, record the date, and make notes of specific observations of the student's work that day.

- Fill a three-ring binder with notebook paper and a divider for each student. Then use sticky notes to jot down observations during small-group work and attach them to pages in the correct sections of the notebook.

- Create a recipe file box with one file for each student. Take notes on small notecards of observations made during small-group work and file them accordingly. Use separate note cards for each student.

Whatever system a teacher chooses to use, it is important to keep these records. The specific feedback teachers give students during the lesson is a valuable source of data. When this is recorded and saved, it will guide future instruction, provide documentation of progress, indicate students who need additional interventions, and can also be shared with parents during conferences.

Select the Next Steps for Instruction

Using the anecdotal notes for each group, teachers should reflect on the learning that has been demonstrated by the students in the group and on the misconceptions or areas in which additional work is needed. Obviously, if students were very successful with the activity or task, it's time to move on to another area of instruction, based on the curriculum sequence established by the teacher, school, or district.

When most of the students struggle with the work, it's time to go back and present it in a different way or break it down into smaller, more manageable components. Sometimes, students just need additional time exploring the concept before it really makes sense to them. If the notes indicate some obvious points of misunderstanding, the teacher can focus instruction on them. Teachers can use their professional judgment to determine the most efficient and effective lessons to teach any concepts with which students struggle.

Each group will have its own unique needs—needs that may not have been apparent until the end of a unit with a traditional method of instruction—which can now be immediately addressed so that all students move forward at the appropriate pace in their mathematical instruction.

Identify Students Who Are Falling Behind

In spite of small-group instruction, some students may still fall behind. Teachers, aware of the demands to successfully teach the entire mathematics curriculum to each student, are torn between the desire to move these students forward even if they haven't established foundational understandings for the work to come and the recognition that these students really need to build those foundations first.

Unfortunately, there is no cure-all that will completely remedy this situation. It is one that almost every teacher faces at some time or another. Clearly, students will not be successful without strong foundational understandings. But, it is equally clear that if they don't even experience the grade-level curriculum, there is no way they can be successful with it.

In some school systems, these students receive "double dips" of mathematics instruction. This can be achieved in several ways. If students participate in art activities, they can receive additional mathematics lessons during that time with either their homeroom teachers or with other designated teachers. Another option is having students go to other classrooms for additional instruction during mathematics time in those classrooms, as long as they will not miss reading or math instruction in their regular classrooms. The drawback with these plans is the students miss either art or another part of the curriculum, perhaps science or social studies. Knowing the importance of mathematics for success in middle school and high school, some schools believe it is a priority.

Within the classroom, teachers can also address the challenge by pulling these students for individual mini lessons whenever possible—sometimes, first thing in the morning or as the rest of the class works independently. Although this tends to be hit-or-miss instruction, it is extra instruction, and every bit helps.

Of course, as the struggles of these students are documented, some of them will be eligible for special programs. Small-group instruction allows teachers to become aware of specific areas of need early. Consistent documentation helps these students obtain additional assistance if they qualify for it.

A final suggestion is the use of peer tutors, tutors from a higher grade level, or adult tutors. With tutors, the instruction may not be the quality the students' teachers would provide, but it can help. The relationships that develop in these tutoring sessions can also boost the confidence of struggling learners and provide mentors for the students.

Change the Composition of the Groups

As teachers review the notes from the small-group lessons, they may find that a student has suddenly achieved a level of understanding that goes beyond that of the other students in the group, or conversely, that a student seems to be lagging behind the others. When teachers note this, it's wise to wait at least until after another lesson with the group to make a change. If it appears that the performance of these students is consistent, it's time to move the student to a more appropriate group. Students, as well as teachers, should recognize that the composition of the groups is fluid and changes based on need. Students have opportunities to change groups as their academic needs change. If there are no appropriate groups available, teachers can either try to vary instruction within a group or work individually with those students, whenever possible.

A Sample Small-Group Lesson

Let's return to our hypothetical student Nina, whose next learning steps were described earlier in the chapter. She was able to recognize equivalent fractions, but not able to generate them. The teacher is now grouped with several other students who are in the same situation. Her teacher has designed a lesson to scaffold their learning so they can generate equivalent fractions.

Nina's teacher begins by reminding students that they have been working with fractions. The teacher points to the vocabulary card posted behind the small-group table that has the words "equivalent fractions" on it, along with the definition. The students read it aloud.

Using 12 two-color counters, the teacher turns four of them so the red side is on top, while the other eight have the yellow side up. Initially, she puts out the four red counters.

Thinking aloud, the teacher says, *"Let's see—I have four red counters. I wonder what fractional part of all my 12 counters that is? How can I answer that question? To begin, I know I have 12 counters, so each of them is 1/12. Since four of them are red, 4/12 are red. That means 8/12 are yellow. I didn't even have to count them because I already know that four and eight added together equals 12. I wonder if 4/12 is equivalent to another fraction. Maybe I can separate the counters into equal groups. Okay, what if I start with the four I have? The reds make one group of four. Can I make groups of four with the other counters?"*

The teacher groups the yellow counters into groups of four.

"Well, I have two groups of four yellow counters. Altogether, there are three groups now. If I want to use the groups to find the fractional parts, one of the three groups is red or 1/3 of the counters are red. Two of the three groups are yellow—so 2/3 of the counters are yellow. Ummm…I still have 12 counters. I still have four reds and eight yellows. So, if in the first instance, the reds make up 4/12, and then when in groups of four, they make up 1/3, 4/12 and 1/3 must be equivalent fractions."

The teacher monitors the expressions of the students to be sure they are following her reasoning before continuing.

"Can you help me now? I found that 4/12 and 1/3 are equivalent. Do you remember what fractional part of the whole eight was?"

A student responds correctly.

"You are right. The eight yellow counters make up 8/12 of the counters. Look at the groups of four. Using those groups, can you name another fraction that is equivalent to 8/12?"

Three students respond with the correct answer, *2/3.*

"Can you think of another way we could divide the 12 counters into equal groups?"

One of the students suggests groups of five. They try it and find it doesn't work because some are left over. Another student suggests groups of two. They divide the counters into groups of two successfully.

"How many groups are there now?"

Students count and answer six.

"Can you name another fraction that is equivalent to 4/12 and 1/3?"

One student volunteers the answer *2/6*.

"How did you know that fraction is equivalent to 1/3 and 4/12?"

The student correctly answers that there are still 12 counters and four of them are still red. Even though they are grouped differently, the fractions are equivalent if they are representations for the same amount or quantity. The teacher asks the other students to restate that in their own words.

Then, the teacher gives each pair of students 16 linking cubes, four of which are red and 12 of which are blue, and asks the students to tell what fractional part the blues represent. The students do this easily. The teacher makes note of this on the recording sheet.

Next, the teacher asks the students to name a fraction that is equivalent to 12/16. Immediately, two groups of students begin to divide their cubes into equal groups.

A third pair of students seems stuck and doesn't know how to proceed. The teacher asks them to describe the previous demonstration with the counters. As they recall the process, one of them suddenly thinks of a strategy for finding an equivalent fraction. He shares it with his partner. *"Let's divide them into groups of two."* The partner responds, *"Why groups* of two?" "I chose groups of two because I think the counters will divide evenly into groups of two."

They begin working. The teacher makes notes about these two students to remind herself that they weren't quite ready to work independently.

One pair of students very quickly divide the cubes into four groups of four. As the teacher listens to the pair's discussion, they name 3/4 as an equivalent fraction to 12/16. The teacher asks that pair to find another equivalent fraction and then to record in their Math Journals what they learn.

A second pair of students try to divide the cubes into groups of eight. They divide them successfully, but then struggle with what to do since one group was composed of both red and blue cubes. The teacher listens for a few minutes as the students discuss their dilemma. When they seem stymied, the teacher asks them to think about the work with the counters.

"What did you notice about the groups? How did the groups with the counters differ from your groups of cubes?"

After thinking for a few minutes, one of the students answers, "The groups of counters were either all red or all yellow."

After waiting for a few minutes to give the pair a chance to think of what its next step would be, the teacher asks, "What do you think you could do to find the equivalent fraction?"

One of them says, "Oh, I guess the groups have to be all one color or the other, right?" They go on to create groups of four in which the groups contain only one color and are able to name an equivalent fraction correctly. They are asked to record in their Math Journal what they did to find equivalent fractions.

The group who struggled at first finally finished creating groups of two where each group was composed of only a single color. They surprised the teacher by being able to name the equivalent fraction 6/8. They were also asked to record their work in their Math Journals.

When the students finish writing, the teacher asks Nina to share what they had done during the lesson. She begins to explain, but is more focused on the grouping than on making the connection to finding an equivalent fraction. Another of the students begins to explain his understanding by verbally going through the process from the beginning again. The teacher brings their attention back to the definition of an equivalent fraction. Eventually, one student is able to explain why she knew the fractions were equivalent—because they are different names for the same amount.

The teacher is pleased that they made some progress with this lesson, but feels that the group needs a little more experience creating equivalent fractions with concrete objects. The teacher decides to provide a variety of manipulatives in the next lesson and allow the students to choose which they will use. Observations will be made to see what they do if they choose more than two different color objects with which to work. The teacher places anecdotal notes in each student's file. Upon reflecting on the lesson, the teacher decides that these students still seemed to have similar instructional needs, so no changes in grouping will be necessary before the next lesson.

Chapter Snapshot

Teaching students in small groups provides benefits for both teachers and students. The intimate setting allows teachers to target students' instructional needs and is conducive to exploration, conversation, and discovery. When teachers meet with small groups, students clamor to be included. Teachers learn about their students—how they think, how they express themselves, how they work together, and how they learn. Knowing this, teachers can scaffold the learning of their students and provide them with specific feedback.

Review and Reflect

1. How does using flexible, needs-based grouping affect student learning? How can it affect teaching strategies employed by teachers?

2. Do you use Guided Reading in your classroom? If so, how can you adapt it to accommodate mathematics instruction? What about it is easily modified for teaching mathematics? What may be more difficult to adapt?

3. What data do you have that can guide you as you create small groups of students for Guided Math instruction?

1 2 3
4 5 **6**
7 8 9

Supporting Guided Math with Math Workshop

In sharp contrast to the teacher-directed model of instruction, the Math Workshop component of Guided Math shifts much of the responsibility for learning to the students. Math Workshop has its origins in the math centers of the 1970s. Students in primary grades explored math concepts using familiar objects to build strong understandings of the patterns of mathematics. Students learned at work stations with tasks designed to give them ample opportunities to explore a wide range of mathematical concepts. Teachers relied on *Mathematics Their Way,* created and written by Mary Barrata-Lorton (1976), for guidance in planning the center activities that built sequentially throughout the year.

Giving students foundational experiences working with concrete objects eased their transitions to symbolic and abstract representation. Barrata-Lorton reminds teachers that, "Abstract symbolization is only used to label a concept which the child already grasps, never as a 'material' from which a child is taught a concept" (1976). As teachers recognized the truth of her statement, the use of math centers in primary grades proliferated. As students grew older, however, their instruction most often became more traditional and abstract. While some students were able to make transitions to more abstract thought with success, others struggled with few opportunities to return to the concrete or symbolic (pictorial) to strengthen their understanding.

Coinciding with the increased use of math centers was the implementation of writing workshops in many classrooms (Calkins 1994, Fletcher and Portalupi 2001). With mini lessons, followed by time for students to write independently as teachers conferred with individual writers, writing workshops motivated students to begin taking more responsibility for their writing. It was not long before innovative teachers began using a similar workshop structure for reading instruction. Soon, teachers realized that teaching students to work independently allowed them opportunities to work with small groups of students.

With the adoption of rigorous mathematics standards, there has been a reemergence of interest in instructional approaches that both deepen students' understanding and also bolster the ability of students to work independently. Teachers who have been using writing and reading workshops in their classrooms naturally turn to the workshop model to enhance their mathematics instruction. Now, this approach can be used in primary and secondary grades. The independent activities used in Math Workshop today may not always be the same as those in the centers in the 1970s, but they are activities that students can complete independently—individually, in pairs, or in groups.

Advantages of Math Workshop

Math Workshop is a versatile structure that accommodates a vast array of learning activities. Its flexibility is one of its greatest advantages. Students may work individually, in pairs, or other groupings, depending upon the task or tasks to be completed. The independent work assigned may be investigations, paper-and-pencil activities, math-fact practice, mathematical games, explorations, problem solving, Math Journal writing, computer practice or interactive games, or activities related to other content areas.

With reading and writing instruction, teachers have learned the value in giving students some choice in what they write and what they read. When students are given choices, they take more ownership of their learning experiences. The Math Workshop format offers opportunities for teachers to provide choices of mathematics activities for their students.

Giving students choices during Math Workshop is one way of differentiating instruction for students. They may make their choices based on interests or learning styles. In general, Math Workshop is designed to build on each student's strengths and needs.

It is important for teachers to help students develop the ability to work with endurance on assigned tasks without repeated reminders to stay on task. As students learn to function in Math Workshop, they should be given the responsibility for understanding exactly what the tasks are, clarifying directions, if necessary, and then carrying out whatever they need to do to accomplish their assignments. If the school experiences of students consist solely of assignments where procedures are prescribed and teachers are available at any time for questions and clarifications, they will fail to perceive the necessity of listening carefully to the expectations for the work and looking ahead to anticipate questions they may have or needs they may encounter. When students realize that they will have to work independently for an extended period of time, they begin to develop these vital life skills. These are precisely the kinds of 21st-century skills that employers are looking for, but are not explicitly found in curriculum standards. With the Math Workshop format, students encounter tasks that not only encourage the development of conceptual understanding, but also the work habits that will lead to their future successes.

When students work in groups during Math Workshop, they learn how to work together collaboratively with shared purposes. Expectations set forth by the teacher prior to group work let students know that each group member is expected to contribute and that all members are to be treated respectfully. Cooperative group work teaches students how to communicate effectively, to assume joint responsibility, and to share any materials needed for their work.

In addition to the intrinsic benefits of students participating in Math Workshop, using Math Workshop permits teachers to work with small groups or to confer with students while the remaining students are involved with meaningful learning experiences. Because small-group work is such a valuable component of an instructional program, this advantage is huge. Most often the alternatives to using Math Workshop are forsaking small-group instruction or having students complete "busy work" while the teacher is working with small groups.

Challenges of Math Workshop

For Math Workshop to work well, student procedures and expectations must be considered carefully and then taught to the students. Unless learners understand that their work must be completed independently, they will continually call upon their teachers for help. If teachers anticipate possible student needs and set up procedures so students know what to do to meet those needs, the workshop will run smoothly. Without this forethought, Math Workshop can be chaotic. It does take extra time and effort to put these procedures in place.

It is important to plan an effective Math Workshop. Because there are so many options available to teachers, choosing which to use first can be difficult, especially when teachers are just getting started. Like dining at a fine restaurant where the entrees described on the menu are all so enticing, each with its own unique appeal, Math Workshop's instructional options are many, but choices must be made. For teachers who are implementing Math Workshop for the first time, it is often initially wise to limit the range of activities and find out what works well for them.

The time required to plan Math Workshop may be lengthier than planning a traditional mathematics lesson—especially in the first year of implementation. Selecting the tasks is the first step. Part of the preparation may include preparing materials for multiple activities, as well as establishing the criteria for success for those activities. With experience, teachers can build collections of resources that can be used periodically throughout the year, and then the resources can be used year after year, making the planning and preparation process easier. When teachers work collaboratively, they can share their resources and divide up the preparation of materials so that no one teacher is responsible for planning and preparing all the activities for Math Workshop.

Due to the independent nature of the Math Workshop assignments and the fact that teachers are occupied with small groups or conferring with students, student work may not be monitored closely. For that reason, some of the best tasks that can be completed during Math Workshop are listed below.

- review previously mastered concepts
- practice for math fact automaticity
- use mathematical games to reinforce concepts
- practice problem solving
- investigate mathematical concepts
- write in Math Journals
- complete computer-related work
- complete math-related work from other subject areas
- complete work from small-group instruction

Effective Uses for Math Workshop

Figure 6.1 Math Workshop Components

Component	Review of Previously Mastered Concepts	Math Fact Automaticity	Math Games	Problem-Solving Practice
Objectives	• Ensures retention of understanding of concepts previously achieved by students	• Increases computational proficiency of students through math fact fluency	• Reinforces math standards being taught currently and which have been taught to students prior to Math Workshop	• Requires the use of strategies or related to concepts previously modeled, taught, and practiced
Examples	• hands-on activities • problems to solve • games • activity sheets • computer activities	• flash cards • games • computer activities • activity sheets • timed tests	• commercially prepared games • games suggested by teacher editions of textbooks • teacher created games	• problems of the day • problems of the week

Figure 6.1 Math Workshop Components *(cont.)*

Component	Investigations	Math Journals	Computer Use	Math Related to Other Subject Areas
Objectives	• Similar to problem-solving practice, but requires the gathering of data or other information by students	• Enhances mathematical process skills	• Supports the understanding of math concepts • Provides practice to promote math fluency • Provides resources for investigation and for creation of presentation of findings	• Helps students realize the interrelatedness of the disciplines • Focuses on the real-life applications of math
Examples	• real-life, relevant investigations provided by the teacher or generated by students	• response to teacher prompts • mathematical observations • definitions of math-specific vocabulary • recording of conjectures • log of problem-solving steps or strategies • explanation of mathematical understanding	• math games • math tutorial programs • Internet research for investigations • *PowerPoint®* or other multimedia presentations related to math	• math activities tied to current events • science projects • math connections from social studies, language arts, and science textbooks

Review Previously Mastered Concepts

Over an academic year, learning is often sequential. One concept builds on another. As students move on to new concepts, they continue to make use of earlier learning, practicing previously mastered skills. Some parts of student learning, however, are more discrete and autonomous. They may be directly addressed several times a year, but may not regularly be used when other parts of the curriculum are being taught. As with learning any concepts, however, if they are not revisited regularly, they may be forgotten.

By assigning activities that require students to work with previously learned concepts during Math Workshop, teachers ensure that their students retain the understanding they achieved earlier in the year and are able to complete the work independently. In some classrooms, during the month or so prior to standardized testing, students in Math Workshop rotate from center to center to review areas of mathematics they have learned earlier in the year. These hands-on tasks at each center give students opportunities to reinforce their earlier learning so it is fresh in their minds when they are challenged with similar problems on the high-stakes tests.

Teachers determine how to best keep their students' skills and understanding sharp. Occasionally, a teacher may accomplish this with something as uncomplicated as an activity sheet. Often, hands-on activities with manipulatives will better serve this purpose. Games are also an excellent way to motivate students to interact with concepts which need to be practiced to be retained.

Practice for Math Fact Automaticity

The U.S. Department of Eduction's *The Final Report of the National Mathematics Advisory Panel* (2008) stresses the importance of sufficient and appropriate practice so that students achieve automaticity with math facts. According to the Panel, computational proficiency with whole-number operations is dependent on students learning their basic math facts. As students develop immediate recall of these facts, they free their working memory for solving more complex problems.

Teachers help students develop strategies for gaining automaticity by focusing students' attention on number relationships. Sometimes, students need time to practice applying these strategies. While some students are fortunate enough to have family and friends who work with them at home as they study these facts, many students don't. Rather than use instructional time when students have direct contact with their teachers, students can work individually or in pairs during Math Workshop to gain math-fact automaticity. Pairs of students can practice these facts by working with flashcards, playing games, or working with specific computer programs aimed at automaticity.

Use Mathematical Games to Reinforce Concepts

Children love games, and teachers have taken advantage of this fact for years. Today, it is easy to find games that reinforce the mathematical standards to be learned. Curriculum companies provide games with their texts, school supply stores sell games, and teacher sites on the Internet abound with ideas for teachers to create their own games.

Before planning to use a game during Math Workshop, there are some things to consider. First, the game should align with the curriculum. It's not good enough to plan to use a game just because it looks as if students would enjoy it and it's related to mathematics. With the instructional demands in place today and the limited amount of time allotted to accomplish them, teachers need to be sure that the games used in class actually help students learn the specific content being taught.

Next, the games should not be too complex and detailed. Games that might be appropriate in a home setting where children would have considerable support as they play may not be a good choice for Math Workshop. Students should be able to understand the rules of the game and manage its components easily. The challenge should be the mathematics required to play it, not the structure of the game itself.

Lastly, before students are asked to play a game independently during Math Workshop, they should be taught to play the game and have either whole-class or small-group time to practice it. During this initial practice time, students should be carefully supervised by teachers or other adults. If students are asked to play a game as a part of Math Workshop without preliminary instruction and practice, its use will most likely prove to be ineffective. If students are not sure of the procedures, they may argue over them or just make up the rules as they go. The resulting confusion may spill over and disrupt small-group work or conferencing.

Games can constitute an effective part of Math Workshop. Because of their potential value, it only makes sense that teachers take time to choose them carefully, introduce them thoroughly, and then provide practice with them before asking learners to work with them independently. By following these steps, teachers set the stage for their effective use as a learning tool.

Practice Problem Solving

Teachers in many classrooms challenge students with Problems of the Day or Problems of the Week. These problems are sometimes posed as morning work or included in the daily calendar-board activities. After problem-solving procedures and strategies for problem solving have been modeled and demonstrated in those contexts, students may be ready to work independently on a Problem of the Day or Problem of the Week as a part of Math Workshop.

The selection of the problems to be presented to students is not always easy. Students should encounter problems more complex than those traditionally found in textbooks. The traditional textbook word problems focus on requiring students to translate specified situations into arithmetic sentences where there is usually just one way to solve each problem and one correct answer (Burns 2000). In real life, however, problems are rarely so simple. One must call upon mathematical and nonmathematical knowledge, previous experiences, and often intuition. While not minimizing the importance of the mathematics necessary to solve problems, more demanding problems also require students to think deeply and call upon skills that they will need in real life as they are faced with problems.

How do teachers choose meaningful problems for students? Marilyn Burns (2000) offers these criteria of mathematical problems:

- There is a perplexing situation that the student understands.
- The student is interested in finding a solution.
- The student is unable to proceed directly toward a solution.
- The solution requires the use of mathematical ideas.

Tying problems to situations that are real and familiar to students sparks their interest and helps them link the problems to their previous experiences and background knowledge. This foundational understanding provides scaffolding as students work toward solving the problems and, through this process, generate new understandings.

When solving a Problem of the Day or Problem of the Week as a part of Math Workshop, a teacher should introduce it to the whole class prior to beginning the workshop. It is essential that students understand the problem before they begin working so the teacher's time with other students will be uninterrupted. Since understanding word problems usually requires reading comprehension skills, some students will need support in being able to understand the facts of the problem and in determining exactly what they are being asked to find. If the teacher has a procedure he or she wants students to follow as they work to solve the problem, it should be made clear to students before they begin their work. Some teachers ask students to use graphic organizers to help them structure their work. Problem solvers may have to state what it is they are trying to find out, what the facts of the problem are, what special conditions exist, what can be done to solve it, what was done to solve it, and the answer in the form of a sentence. Students may also be asked to show multiple representations of their answers.

For problem-solving tasks, students may work alone or in groups. If the task is assigned to groups, it helps if specific roles are given to students. One student may act as a group leader who reads the problem and leads the discussion about how to solve the problem. One student may have the role of recorder. One may be assigned the task of gathering materials the group needs. Another may be designated to handle the materials as the group works to solve the problem. Clarification of specific group roles prevents disagreements within the group, so that its total attention is focused on solving the problem. Whatever the job assignments, teachers should be sure that they are rotated over time so that eventually each student has a chance to perform each job.

Since problem solving is often best accomplished by using manipulatives to model the problem or other materials such as markers, chart paper, graph paper, stickers, glue, or scissors to create representations of the problem, a choice of materials should be readily available to students as they decide how they want to approach solving the problem. Students should know where the materials are kept, what procedures they should follow to get the materials, and then how the materials should be put away when the group is finished using them. To avoid interruption of the small groups or conferences, students should not be dependent on the teacher to get the materials.

Regardless of whether problem solving is an individual or group activity and whether it occurs during a single day or over a period of several days, it's important that students have a chance to reflect on and discuss their work—their thinking about the problem, the processes they used to solve the problem, their solutions, what worked well, and what didn't work so well. Students should be asked to explain their answers whether they are correct or incorrect. The teacher should allow most of the discourse to be by the students themselves, acting only as a facilitator. It's important for the teacher to direct the conversation so that misconceptions are addressed, correct mathematical vocabulary is modeled, and students become aware of mathematical relationships that are evident in their work.

The marriage of problem-solving tasks and Math Workshop is effective. When students are well-prepared for the challenge presented and for what the expectations are for their work habits during the workshop, Math Workshop provides an extended time of mathematical exploration.

Investigate Mathematical Concepts

An investigation is similar to a problem-solving task, but it is usually more extensive and requires gathering data. Students may work on investigations individually or in groups. Procedures and expectations for this work must be clear. A specific investigation may be assigned to the class or students may be allowed to choose from a bank of investigations. Tasks can be written on cards and laminated. When students choose tasks, they can borrow the cards from the Investigations Bank, a box of laminated investigations, to take to their work spaces. They can return the cards when they have completed the tasks. Students are also asked to keep logs that document their work.

Topics for investigations may arise from other content areas. Some of the most valuable investigations arise from questions that students have relating to their own experiences. The following are sample investigation scenarios:

- During election periods, students can investigate a local, state, or national election. Younger students may take polls to determine the number of students supporting each candidate. Older students may take that data to determine the fractional part or percent of the student body supporting each candidate. The investigation could continue by tracking the support for each candidate over time with students computing not only the percentage of support, but also the percentage of change over time with graphic depictions of their data. Students could use the data to predict the outcomes of the races and then check their predictions when they learn the outcome of the election.

- When a teacher is going to purchase materials for the classroom, students might research where they can be purchased least expensively and then compute the total costs, including the shipping.

- In the spring, if the class is planting a garden, students can calculate how many square feet it should be and design layouts after consulting seed packages to determine how far apart different kinds of plants should be planted.

- If a student wondered what plane is the fastest in the world, he or she could lead an investigation to find the fastest plane. The relative speeds of different planes might be graphed.

Teachers who are attuned to the questions students raise find many opportunities to create investigations based on their interests. But, by no means do investigations have to arise from student questions or classroom topics of interest. Problems for investigations are readily available in books, math periodicals, and on websites. Teachers can collaborate and share the task of creating a bank of investigations. Once created, most of them can be used from year to year.

Periodically, during an investigation and at its conclusion, students should have opportunities to reflect on their work, both the procedures and the content. Taking time to discuss their work during the investigation gives students the chance to go back and revise the work as a result of their own reflections or questions from others. Having a conversation when the work is complete offers students who have worked on the same investigation in other groups or on other investigations to learn from each other.

Write in Math Journals

Communication is one of the process standards set forth by NCTM. According to the standards (2000), students should develop the capacity to "use the language of mathematics to express mathematical ideas precisely." For students to develop this ability, they need daily opportunities to both talk and write about mathematics. The use of Math Journals during Math Workshop provides students with meaningful practice and shares their mathematical ideas in writing.

Math Journals may be used by students to record mathematical observations, to record the meanings of mathematics vocabulary words, to write about conjectures they have made, to log steps they used in problem solving, and to write about their understanding of mathematical concepts. In organizing their thoughts for writing, students may discover questions they have or inconsistencies in their thinking. The reflections they go through when planning their writing and the actual physical process of writing their mathematical ideas also help students retain the information that they are learning.

During Math Workshop, students may write in their Math Journals during or after finding the solutions to problems or investigations. Or, the journal writing may be a task in and of itself. To spur student reflection, teachers can assign specific questions for students to address. Student responses to broad, open-ended questions such as, "What did you learn today?" or "What questions do you have?" are frequently disappointing. Students answering these questions tend to describe what they did rather than reflect on their learning, or else they are reluctant to admit that there may be something they don't understand. Instead, Whitin and Whitin (2000) suggest the following questions:

1. What do you notice?

2. What do you find interesting?

3. What patterns do you see?

4. What surprises you?

5. What do you predict? Why?

6. What do your findings make you wonder?

7. What does this remind you of?

These questions invite children "to look closely, find interesting things, detect patterns, predict outcomes, pursue surprises, and pose wonders" (Whitin and Whitin 2000). Students do not need to respond to each question daily. Rather, teachers should ask students to respond to a question that seems appropriate based on the mathematics the students are writing about.

However Math Journals are used, to be most effective, teachers should read the writings of their students carefully and respond to them. These responses should include specific descriptive feedback, which tells students what they did well and what they can work on as a next step. For teachers, these writings are assessment tools. They clearly indicate what students know and how well they can communicate their ideas. From the students' own words, the teacher can identify the students' misconceptions and promptly address them.

Complete Computer-Related Work

Technology plays an enormous role in our lives and in the lives of today's students. Even students who don't have computers at home have experience with computerized games. Because of their affinity for computer games, students are highly motivated and engaged when they are practicing mathematical skills on computers.

Teachers who are fortunate enough to have a bank of computers in their classrooms can use Math Workshop in a variety of ways. Students who need some extra practice with mathematical skills may be assigned to computers to work on programs geared to their needs. Students that struggle to attain automaticity with math facts can be assigned to programs that turn the practice into games. Other computer software programs assist student learning through tutorials tailored to the achievement levels of individual students. In addition, students who are working on investigations may find information they need on the Internet. As with any other instructional resource, teachers should choose computer programs that align with the curriculum being learned, and be sure that students know how to use these resources properly before they use them for independent work.

Complete Math-Related Work from Other Subject Areas

In the real world, unless one happens to be a mathematician, mathematics is rarely something encountered in isolation. We deal with numbers in connection with shopping or checking our bank account statements. Teachers work with numbers as we compute grades. The news we read or listen to is replete with numbers that help us understand the world around us. Too often, our students see mathematics as a discipline totally separate from the rest of their lives.

It is important for teachers to help students grasp the enormous role that mathematics plays in our world. To some extent, teachers can do this within language arts, science, and social studies lessons.

But, teachers can also plan for math-related language arts, science, and social studies work to be included in Math Workshop. Not only do students begin to comprehend the function of mathematics in their world, but this practice gives the teacher additional time for instruction in other content areas.

Complete Work from Small-Group Instruction

Teachers who work with small groups quickly realize how valuable that time is. With so many student needs and so little time, teachers try to maximize time spent with those who need help the most without neglecting the needs of their other students. One way they can do this is by allowing students to complete small-group tasks independently once they demonstrate their understanding.

So, when teachers meet with a small group to introduce a new concept and then have students practice it, they may not need to have the students stay in the group until the practice work is complete. Once the concept is introduced and group members begin to practice, the teacher can monitor the students' work closely for a few minutes. Students who demonstrate understanding can be allowed to leave the group and complete the activity or task independently in Math Workshop. Those who need additional support remain in the group until the teacher is confident that they understand the concept. By dismissing students to work independently, teachers can work more closely with any students who are struggling. Additionally, the amount of time spent with groups can vary based on how quickly students show their understanding.

For example, a teacher may plan to work with three groups during a one-hour mathematics class. The groups have been determined by the instructional needs of the students. The teacher chooses to work first with a group that has quickly demonstrated understanding of the basic concepts being taught. The teacher wants to move them to their next instructional step during small-group work. With a mini lesson, the new concept is introduced, and then students are given an activity for practice. As the teacher informally assesses the students' work, it is apparent that they understand the new concept. They can return to Math Workshop to complete the task and will then begin their other Math Workshop activities. Although the teacher has allocated a longer time to spend with the group, if needed, the extra time can now be spent with the remaining two groups.

The second group has greater instructional needs. The mini lesson is presented with a little more scaffolding to support students' understanding. Then these students will begin the assigned activity. Two of the six students quickly demonstrate their understanding and leave the group to work independently. The teacher can provide some additional instruction for the other four members of the group. The teacher should monitor their work until he or she is satisfied that they are able to work independently. Then students can return to Math Workshop to complete the assigned work before beginning their other workshop assignments. Even with the extra instruction for the four students, this group's lesson took less time than the teacher had planned.

Now, the teacher can begin to work with the group with the greatest instructional needs. Because the first two groups took less time than planned, more time can be spent with these students. With this group, not only is the mini lesson longer and more supportive, but also most of these students will remain with the teacher as they complete their tasks. Two of the six students in this group demonstrated their understanding after the mini lesson and returned to Math Workshop to complete their tasks independently. The teacher is now able to work very closely with the four remaining students, supporting their learning in a more intensive manner.

By taking advantage of the flexibility of the Guided Math framework, this teacher was able to plan instruction that gave the higher-level students information that was specifically tailored to their needs, while at the same time providing additional support for the struggling students.

Managing Math Workshop

Strong classroom management is essential for Math Workshop

to be implemented. Before students are expected to be responsible for independently managing their time and behavior during the workshop framework, teachers must reflect on exactly how they want their students to behave during Math Workshop and then explicitly teach these behaviors. By establishing and teaching guidelines that help the class function independently, teachers help students learn self-management skills.

These self-management skills are not only building blocks for individual student achievement, but are also the foundation for creating a genuine learning community in which students can work collaboratively together. Fountas and Pinnell (2001, 88) list the following principles on which a learning community is based:

- All members are trusted with rights and responsibilities.
- All members take responsibility for their own learning and for helping others to learn.
- All members take responsibility for managing their time and activities productively.
- All members learn self-management as part of the curriculum delivered by the teachers.
- All members understand that keeping materials in order helps everyone learn.

These principles reflect a common-sense approach to managing Math Workshop, and workshop rules or guidelines should promote them. Most teachers would agree with these principles. To have a successful Math Workshop, however, students must understand and accept these principles. It is not always easy to know how to teach the principles to students in a meaningful way. Sometimes, it helps teachers to see what other teachers do in their classrooms. If they have opportunities, teachers can visit each other's classrooms to see how they are organized for Math Workshop. Often, it's helpful for teachers to discuss their workshop rules and expectations with each other, especially at the beginning of the school year.

The behavior of students in Math Workshop closely reflects

the degree of organization in the classroom. The responsibility for creating this well-organized classroom environment rests on the shoulders of the teacher. The teacher needs to have a vision for how his or her classroom will work as students are engaged in independent activities. Once that vision is formulated, the teacher often asks for student involvement in identifying the behavior that positively or adversely affects this collaborative working environment. The solicitation of students' ideas helps them begin to feel they are responsible, contributing members of the community. When the positive and negative behaviors have been identified, the teacher and class can work together to create procedures to support the positive behaviors and prevent the negative behaviors. Drawing upon his or her own visions and upon the suggestions of his or her students, the teacher can guide students as they compile the rules or procedures the students think will prove to be effective when they are working independently. Then these procedures can be stated in a simple, positive manner and posted in the classroom to be referred to whenever needed.

When the workshop guidelines are developed, teachers should explicitly teach them to the class and involve students in discussions about these behavioral and academic expectations. Through the use of modeling and demonstrations, students can see what the expectations "look" like. Then, once the guidelines have been taught to the class, consistency in enforcing them is crucial. During the year, if students begin to become lax in following these procedures, it may be necessary to revisit them or to revise them to fit the evolving needs of the class. Math Workshop runs smoothly when students, by following the guidelines, begin to acquire the self-discipline to monitor their own behavior and work. Then teachers are able to use this instructional time to confer with students individually or to work with small groups without interruption.

During the first few weeks of Math Workshop, procedures may not go as smoothly as teachers would wish. In spite of thoughtful preparation and careful teaching of procedures, there may be some kinks that arise. It helps to try to anticipate problems that may be predictable and have students practice what they will do when they occur. If unpredictable problems arise, it is often helpful for teachers to step back and take time to observe their own classes. Have students engage in Math Workshop activities, but rather than working with small groups or conferring with students, teachers can just observe what is happening in their classrooms as students work. Where are problems arising? More often than not, as teachers act as observers, they can recognize patterns in the problems and are able to find deeper solutions (Calkins, Hartman, and White 2005). Sometimes, solutions may be as simple as rearranging the classroom to create easier access to materials.

These bins are arranged by mathematical concept and contain the necessary supplies for the planned lessons and activities.

Planning with Co-Teachers and Teaching Assistants

Mathematics instruction is a shared responsibility for some teachers. In some classrooms, there are co-teachers or teaching assistants who serve as resources during Math Workshop. These professionals play supportive roles in maintaining atmospheres conducive to learning and in supplementing the instruction of the homeroom or mathematics teachers.

Students with special needs are joining many of today's classrooms. Co-teachers spend portions of each day with the regular education teachers supporting the instructional needs of both special education students and regular education students. There are many ways to implement co-teaching models of instruction, and as co-teachers become accustomed to working together, they soon establish their own instructional styles.

The flexibility of Math Workshop accommodates diverse models of co-teaching. In one possible scenario, both teachers meet with small groups, while the remaining students work independently. Another possible configuration is for one of the teachers to conduct small-group instruction, while the other conferences with students. Alternatively, one teacher may teach a large-group lesson, as the other teacher works with a small group of learners who need specific support. Or, both teachers might be engaged in conferencing with students who are involved in independent work. These are only a few of the feasible instructional combinations.

As co-teachers work together over time and discover each others' strengths, they can explore possible instructional models, which most effectively meet their students' needs and mesh best with their teaching styles. Co-teachers need time to plan together for this to happen. Only when they have time to discuss concerns about their students and construct a common vision regarding daily instruction are they able to work together, flexibly serving the ever-changing needs of their students.

In addition to co-teachers, teaching assistants or paraprofessionals may be assigned full- or part-time to classrooms with special needs students or with younger learners. For teachers who are fortunate enough to have this assistance, the Math Workshop framework becomes even more effective. Teaching assistants can closely supervise the independent work of students to be sure they are on task and have the materials they need. By conferring with students about their work, they can monitor student understanding and correct misconceptions. Teaching assistants should write brief notes about what they observe as they work with students, and then these informal assessments can guide teachers as they plan additional mathematics instruction for these students. Teachers can also take full advantage of having an assistant by sharing the instructional goals and expectations for students during Math Workshop.

Chapter Snapshot

The use of Math Workshop, when it is effectively implemented, teaches students to work independently and assume responsibility for their learning, while at the same time, giving teachers valuable time to confer with learners or to work with students in small groups. Effective implementation means that the work in which students are involved has value. It also means that students are accountable for their work. Consistency in enforcing procedures and rules for independent work ensures that students monitor their own behaviors as they work. The establishment of a well-organized classroom environment allows teachers to successfully implement Math Workshop.

Review and Reflect

1. What are some of the ways that you can organize your classroom to support Math Workshop?

2. How can implementing Math Workshop promote the learning goals you have for your class?

7

Conferring with Students During Guided Math

A visitor to a classroom during Math Workshop may see the teacher move from student to student, seeming to chat informally with each student before moving on to the next. Although it may not be obvious to the visitor, the teacher is involved in an extremely effective instructional tool—conferring. These conversations may appear to be simple "chats," but when done well, the teacher is learning about the students' work, what students understand or are struggling with, and what the next steps in learning should be for both individual students and the class as a whole. Conferring is a fundamental piece of Math Workshop.

In many ways, conferring is the heart and soul of teaching. As we confer with students, we sit alongside them at their levels and listen intently to their words, trying to follow their reasoning and probing to determine the extent of their understanding. According to Calkins, Hartman, and White (2005), "It gives us an endless resource of teaching wisdom, an endless source of accountability, a system of checks and balances. And, it gives us laughter and human connection—the understanding of our children that gives spirit to our teaching."

When we use what we learn from conferring with our students, our instruction becomes more focused and powerful. Conferring with students as they work gives us the timeliest assessments possible. Rather than waiting to see the results of our students' work, we immediately discover their needs as they work. We can address these needs during the conferences, in small groups, with mini lessons, or with whole-class instruction.

It's important for teachers to think through how students will work independently during Math Workshop and how to handle any problems that may arise. Teachers should have clear ideas about how they want their students seated, what they want students to do if they have questions while the teacher is busy, how students will get the supplies they need, and what they envision students will be doing during the workshop. This comprehensive vision is one that will be carried out throughout the entire school year, so it is worth the time and effort it takes to teach these expectations to students until they become second nature to them.

Teachers who are conferring with individual students aren't able to consistently monitor the work of students during the workshop. The tasks assigned should be those that students can do independently. So, what happens when they cannot? If teachers talk with their students about this and let them know that sometimes that may be the case, students are prepared to handle this situation. Calkins, Hartman, and White (2005) suggest telling students in writing workshop that each student is a writing teacher. Students can turn to each other for help when they have questions. In Math Workshop, students can also turn to their peers for assistance. Teachers should have procedures set up so students who hurry through their work and complete a task before the workshop is over know what they should work on next.

Undoubtedly, there may be times when students need some help as they work independently. How can we justify not giving that help when they need it? It's important to keep in mind the value of the targeted teaching that conferring allows teachers to give their students. If teachers are interrupted while conferring, the value of their conferences is diminished. If a student needs help during Math Workshop, rather than interrupting a conference to give stop-gap advice, students participating in a well-planned workshop have guidelines giving them direction as to what they can do independently if problems arise. Later, either that day or the next, the teacher confers with the student who needed assistance specifically addressing his or her needs. During the conference, the teacher has time to more accurately discover what the student's specific problems are and then focus on them. The value of the conference with the student far outweighs the on-the-run direction a teacher may be able to give if interrupted during a conference. When students feel they can interrupt teachers as they confer or meet with small groups, it becomes impossible to effectively use this instructional component.

Moreover, it is important to help students become self-sufficient as they work. Students should know what strategies they can employ when they encounter problems, apart from immediately turning to their teachers. Without these strategies, students can exhibit a "learned helplessness." They immediately ask for help instead of thinking of the options they have and trying to work through the obstacles they believe they face. This may be caused by a lack of confidence, or, sometimes, it may simply be mental laziness on their parts. Too often, students are "spoon-fed" and walked through each step as they solve problems. Because of this support, students fail to develop the endurance to work through problem solving. Consequently, they never experience the satisfaction of solving a problem with which they have struggled. Therefore, when they have to struggle, they quickly become frustrated. When procedures are established to encourage students to assume greater responsibility for their learning, they grow to be more confident and proficient learners.

In addition to students who desire constant teacher support and attention as they work, teachers will inevitably have students who have trouble getting started or staying involved in their work, students who always have needs that require them to be out of their work spaces, or students whose goals are finishing first without regard to the quality of their work. These are the kinds of difficulties that will be encountered, but they are predictable. And because they are predictable, teachers can plan on how to handle them before they occur, or at least before they occur repeatedly.

Teachers who are experienced using Math Workshop find that after students are set to their tasks, they need to spend a few minutes surveying the room to be sure everyone is settling in to his or her assigned task. Often, just being sure that everyone is engaged initially will prevent problems later in the workshop. Students may need a reminder or two of expectations as they begin. Setting the proper tone in the classroom before conferences begin helps ensure uninterrupted time for teachers during conferences.

Initial conferences may be with students who appear to be having a hard time getting started. Management is often easier if teachers crisscross the classroom as they confer, going from one side of the room to the other with each conference, rather than from one student to that student's neighbor. Just the proximity of the teacher keeps some students on task when they are working independently.

If getting materials is a problem, be sure that they are readily available. If a particular student is away from his or her work excessively, try to discover the reason and eliminate it. If the student has a constant need to obtain materials, partner him or her with a more responsible student who will be the only one in that group permitted to get up and get materials.

The conferences are most effective when they occur immediately after teachers observe a behavior in their students. For example, if a student rushes through his or her work, either not completing it or not doing quality work, a teacher can address that behavior in an individual conference. If this is a problem with several students, teachers might meet with them as a small group to reteach and reinforce correct procedures and expectations. Frequent follow-up conferences may be necessary as teachers continue to closely monitor the work of these students. Until they build the self-discipline needed for sustained quality work, they may be asked to work in groups or have clearly designated activities to engage in when they think they have completed assignments.

The Structure of a Conference

When teachers first begin to confer with students, they are sometimes unsure of exactly what they should do. They know that conferring involves conversing with students individually, but wonder precisely what they should do to help their students become more proficient mathematicians. The traditional style of discussion in classrooms is not one normally found in our interactions with our friends and associates. In class, teachers ask questions, call on students, and then let them know if the answer is correct or not. This conversational pattern reinforces the notion that knowledge resides with the teacher to be dispensed to students. The teacher plays an evaluative role, and students recognize this very quickly.

When teachers confer with students, however, the pattern shifts to a sharing of knowledge between students and teachers. Teachers probe to find just what students are thinking, understanding, and wondering. Rather than being afraid to admit that they may be confused, students come to see teachers as partners in their learning journeys. Errors are viewed as valuable steps in these journeys. Carefully crafted questions from teachers encourage students to extend their understanding. Students receive specific descriptive feedback about what they have done well and what they may want to reconsider, and then have opportunities to return to their work, applying their new knowledge.

Calkins, Hartman, and White (2005) propose a consistent architecture for writing conferences that can be adapted effectively to math conferences. This framework guides teachers as they confer with their students, so they can discover what the students are thinking mathematically and then identify what to do to help them progress in their understanding. Following a structure gives purpose to what otherwise may be chatting without focus. Of course, the teachers consider the information they gain through the conversations and use their specific knowledge of the curriculum to determine the teaching points for each student.

In reading instruction, the specific steps for conferences include research, decide, teach, and link (Calkins, Hartman, and White 2005).

When adapted to math conferences, they include:

Research Student Understanding:

- Observe the work of the student and interview him or her to understand what he or she is trying to do as a mathematician. Probe to glean more about the student's intentions.
- Name specifically what the student has done as a mathematician, linking it directly to the language of the standards and remind him or her to do this in future work.

Decide What Is Needed:

- Weigh whether you want to accept or alter the student's current strategies and processes. Decide what you want to teach and how you will teach it.

Teach to Student Needs:

- Use demonstration, guided practice, or explicit telling and showing to correct or extend a student's understanding and ability to successfully complete the task.

Link to the Future:

- Name what the student has done as a mathematician and remind him or her to do this often in the future.

(Adapted from Calkins, Hartman, and White 2005)

When conferring, the teacher should initiate the conversation with a broad general question to spur the student to explain the work in which he or she is engaged. The teacher should listen intently, giving the student his or her entire attention. When the teacher has a good grasp of what the student is attempting, the focus of the conversation shifts to the teacher as he or she begins to teach—the teaching addresses the unique mathematical needs of that student, which were identified during the beginning of the conference. Toward the end of the conference, the teacher and student interact, with the student restating the mathematical teaching point, and the teacher urging the student to always remember to use what he or she has learned.

The teacher provides this student with feedback specific to her progress on the activity.

Research Student Understanding

The goal of a conference is to move a student from what he or she can *almost* do independently to what he or she *can* do independently. This is often a very fine distinction that is not obvious in a finished product. Only by talking with students about their work, questioning, encouraging, and most importantly, listening can teachers discern this distinction. Conferences also bring to light the understanding that students do not all progress at approximately the same rate and respond the same way to the instruction provided.

As students begin working on tasks during Math Workshop, the teacher may already have chosen some students with whom to conference. If not, a glance around the classroom observing the work of students and a few minutes of listening to the discussions of students working in groups help a teacher choose students who may benefit the most from conferences. These may not always be the students who are struggling. Sometimes, it may be students who quickly demonstrate a deep understanding of a concept and need additional challenges.

With whomever teachers choose to confer, the crucial first step is research—finding out what the student is doing with the assigned task and what his or her understandings about the applicable mathematical concepts are. Although the conference itself is very brief, paradoxically, this is a time for teachers to slow down. The research phase is primarily a time for "deep" listening (Fletcher and Portalupi 2001), so teachers can view their students' work products through the students' own lenses. Learning how students perceive their work helps teachers as they choose the most important next learning steps. For many teachers, this may be the most challenging aspect of conferring. From a few minutes of conversation with a student, how can one be confident that the teaching point one chooses is the best one? Perhaps it helps to know that there is rarely one right lesson, and if there is one, it will usually be quite obvious. Different teachers conferring with the same students may decide on different teaching points for very valid reasons based on what they discovered during the research phase. Each of the teaching points may help lead the student to greater understanding.

Teachers who are just beginning the process of conferring should not let concerns over determining the next steps in learning prevent them from carrying out conferences with their students. Only by getting started can they hone their research skills. As teachers gain experience conferring, their confidence will grow.

During the research phase of a conference, teachers are searching for evidence of the mathematical understanding a student has acquired and if the student can apply that understanding appropriately. Entering the conference, teachers already have bodies of knowledge upon which to draw. Sometimes, it is helpful to pause prior to initiating a conference with a student to reflect on what is already known about a given student. Teachers may want to refer to anecdotal notes or other assessment data to refresh their recollections about the student's previous mathematical work. Where has he or she demonstrated mastery? In what areas has he or she struggled? Being aware of the student's past mathematical achievement allows teachers to discern the student's growth in understanding.

Teachers may also recall the learning styles of the students with whom they are going to confer. Do they work best with visual representations? Do kinesthetic activities support their learning most effectively? Do they work well with other students or do they do better working on their own? What do they tend to do if they don't understand problems? The reflection process may not include each of these questions. It only lasts for a moment, but by having some additional information about students prior to conferences, teachers can more easily understand what's going on with the students with whom they confer.

Once a teacher takes a moment to consider what is already known about a student, he or she may want to simply observe the student at work for another moment. Does the student work confidently or seem confused? Is the student working productively or doing everything but what he or she should be working on? What strategies does the student appear to be employing to deal with the assigned task? Are those strategies being used properly? What might the student be overlooking? The observation only takes a minute or so, but it can prepare a teacher to successfully confer with the student.

When teachers join students to begin conferring, they can see the work of the students, whether the work is the use of manipulatives, drawing illustrations, writing number sentences, or explaining mathematical thinking through writing. Teachers may want to scan the work prior to beginning a discussion with students. The initial view of the students' work may give teachers a direction to pursue as they gather research.

To obtain a more in-depth understanding, a teacher can ask broad, general questions about the work of the student or more specific, probing questions based upon the information he or she has put together while reflecting and observing. Experienced teachers recognize that students cannot always put into words the understanding they possess or accurately describe how they are applying what they know. As teachers talk with students, often restating the students' ideas while using mathematical vocabulary, they model useful forms of mathematical communication. Teachers need to be careful when probing to differentiate between the authentic ideas of students and those that are automatic answers to leading questions.

Calkins, Hartman, and White (2005) warn about problems that teachers may face when conducting research during a conference:

- The research phase takes up too much of the time devoted to a conference.
- The research is not used to determine the next steps in learning.

Especially when teachers are beginning to confer with students for the first time, they may devote excessive amounts of time to research. There is so much that can be learned with each conference. But, it is important to balance the amount of time spent on each component of the conference, in order to make it as effective as possible. Gradually, teachers learn to take in and assess the many aspects of their students' work almost as second nature, allowing students ample time to talk, but guiding the discussion away from areas that won't extend their knowledge of their students' levels of understanding.

The second problem is by far the more serious. To be sure, there will be times for all teachers when the research does not dictate the teaching point. Sometimes, it may be difficult to determine just what a student needs. When the lack of connection between research and teaching point occurs on a regular basis, though, it indicates a failure to comprehend the purpose of conferences. The value of conferring with students is in the teacher's ability to pinpoint instructional needs and then to teach short, individualized lessons to target those needs. It is good practice for all teachers to occasionally examine their conferences to be sure the teaching is matched to the research most of the time.

Decide What Is Needed

The decide phase of a conference occurs almost simultaneously with the research phase. As teachers conduct research, they are also gauging students' progress, the strategies used, and students' overall understanding as compared to their learning goals. Teachers are also trying to determine how to most effectively support students' growth. Teachers have three responsibilities during this phase.

1. They identify things students are doing well so that they can give them genuine and specific compliments.

2. They decide what they can teach students to move them forward.

3. They focus on how to best use the few minutes left of the conference to teach those points to the students, so that students' learning will be retained by them and then used in their mathematics work in the future.

Just as informal assessment is instrumental in helping teachers determine where their students are on their journeys toward established instructional goals, it can be used to help students appreciate precisely what they have achieved. Whenever they confer, teachers should make points of noticing the ways in which their students have been successful and then give students authentic, specific compliments based on these accomplishments. The compliments not only confirm to students that they are progressing, but spotlight things that they should continue to do in the future. By focusing compliments on particular activities or achievements, students are motivated to repeat their actions.

Just as teachers are sometimes reluctant to have someone come into their classrooms to critique their teaching, students often feel vulnerable when teachers approach them for conferences. Some students may know they haven't been on task, but most of them have been doing their best. If their assigned work is of value, they should be challenged by it. They may be trying strategies they are not sure about. Having a teacher approach to chat about their work is a little intimidating to some of them. Teachers tend to notice those things that are incorrect or need improvement first. Then they want to take whatever steps are necessary to be sure the work is corrected or improved. However, before this happens, students need to know what they are doing well. When they know that the teacher recognizes those achievements, they are more open to suggestions as teachers move ahead with the teaching points.

Often, compliments can be the entries into teaching points. Once teachers identify compliments for students, the focus turns to choosing teaching points. The more thoroughly teachers know the curriculum, the easier it is to break the knowledge down into a series of teaching points which build on one another in helping students achieve mastery of the standards being taught. With new teachers or with a new curriculum, this process requires considerable thought. It can be difficult to determine exactly what students need next from a few minutes of research at the beginning of conferences. As tempting as it may be to leap to teaching points without completing the research phase, it is necessary to wait patiently to fully understand their students' level of understanding before committing to the next steps in learning. At best, the teaching points provide students with strategies or increased understandings that will remain with them and will be something they will use as they engage in mathematical thinking and problem solving in the future. Teachers should also bear in mind that there is no one correct teaching point for any particular conference. Using what is known of the student and the curriculum, teachers decide and teach. If the teaching proves to be ineffective, there will be other opportunities to reteach and address the needs of that student.

The final component of the decide phase is to choose a method for teaching the next step during the conference. Given the limited amount of time available to teach, deciding what teaching method will most effectively convey the message of the lesson is important. Just telling a student what he or she needs to know is not sufficient.

Teach to Student Needs

After deciding what to teach and how to teach it during the brief time span of a conference, the next phase of a conference is the teaching itself. Drawing on transcriptions of hundreds of writing conferences, Calkins, Hartman, and White (2005) identified three teaching methods that were most often used by teachers:

- guided practice
- demonstration
- explaining and showing an example

These three methods are as effective for teaching mathematics lessons as they are for writing. So, when teachers are in the deciding phase, they will most likely choose one of these methods.

Guided Practice

Students learn best when they are actively involved. What they do remains with them longer than what they hear. When teachers use guided practice, they have students actually practice what is being taught. As students try the strategies on the mathematical tasks on which they are working, teachers are right there alongside them coaching. This ensures that students begin using the strategies they are being taught and that as they make these initial attempts, they are using them correctly. Using guided practice, teachers are able to scaffold the next steps in the learning experiences for their students.

For example, Marisol is a student who is gathering data about which of three field trip possibilities students in her class prefer. The task is a meaningful one because the data is going to be used to help Marisol's teacher plan the next field trip. After Marisol has worked on the project for a while, her teacher notices that she seems to be stuck and so decides to confer with her. Marisol explains that she has gone from student to student, asking them for their preferences. She has neatly listed each student's name and field trip choice. At this point, she is unsure of how to organize the information to find out what it tells about the preferences of the class.

In an earlier mini lesson, the teacher had shown the class how to use a tally chart to organize data. The teacher reminds Marisol of how tally charts can be used and asks her to begin creating one using the information she has already gathered. The teacher observes Marisol's work as she draws a chart and begins to record the data using tallies.

When the teacher sees Marisol record the fifth tally as a vertical line rather than a diagonal line, she reminds Marisol that the fifth tally mark is recorded in a different way. She lets Marisol know that mathematicians who work with tallies always record every fifth mark as a diagonal line going across the previous four vertical lines to create obvious groups of five, making it easier to count how many tallies there are altogether. The teacher watches as Marisol corrects her recording and remains long enough to see Marisol record the next fifth tally correctly. Before concluding the conference, the teacher asks Marisol to always remember that the use of tally charts is one way mathematicians organize data. She may not always choose to make a tally chart, but it is one option she should consider.

In this example of conferencing using guided practice, the teaching point was using tally charts to organize data. The teacher explicitly told Marisol how tally charts are used and then coached her through her first effort at using a tally chart. The teacher was right there to support her initial efforts. When she began to record tallies incorrectly, the teacher stepped in to coach her and help her record tallies properly.

This is just one example of how a teacher may use guided practice to teach the next steps in learning during conferences. Students are involved in trying the teaching points, while teachers provide coaching. Talk by the teacher is minimal as the focus is on the work of the student.

Demonstration

Learning from demonstration seems to be hardwired into our systems. Just watch young siblings. The younger child constantly mimics the older sibling—"monkey see, monkey do." Although the younger child may not be conscious of learning, there is little doubt that demonstrations by the older child teach the younger one. Sometimes, they teach things we'd rather younger children not learn.

Demonstration can be almost as effective when used in conferring with students. As teachers confer with students, they may choose to model mathematics strategies or processes, thinking aloud as they do. When modeling, it helps if teachers break down tasks into achievable steps and explain the reasoning behind each of the steps as they model. By demonstrating processes or strategies, teachers help students see how they look, which helps them as they attempt to replicate them. Demonstrations should conclude with an emphasis on what it is that students should notice or remember from the lessons and with teachers encouraging students to always consider these lessons when they work as mathematicians.

Jamari was struggling to solve a written problem. Through research at the beginning of a conference, his teacher discovered that Jamari could read the problem and knew what he was being asked to find. But, Jamari seemed to be jumping directly into problem solving without taking time to identify the relevant facts in the problem. The teacher decided to use a demonstration to teach Jamari to reread the problem carefully and pick out the important facts before trying to solve it.

The teacher explains, *"Whenever I have a problem to solve, first, I think about what it is I need to find out. You've already done that with this problem. Next, I want to be sure I know what facts are important to know so I can solve it. I'm going to read the problem again carefully and underline the facts. Then I'm going to go back and be sure everything I underlined is needed for this problem."*

The teacher goes through this process, underlines the relevant facts, and then asks, *"Did you notice how I read the problem carefully, underlined the facts, and then went back to recheck them before I tried to actually solve the problem?"*

Finally, the teacher reminds Jamari to be sure to do this each time he has a mathematics problem to solve. In this conference, the demonstration allowed Jamari to see the process the teacher went through as the teacher explained what he was doing. The teacher would want to follow-up with Jamari in the next few days to see if he was able to apply this lesson independently.

Explaining and Showing an Example

In some cases, a teacher may choose to teach a next step by referring a student to an example. The walls of a Guided Math classroom will contain anchor charts showing procedures or strategies the class has discussed, used, and recorded for future reference. As it is solved, a Problem of the Day or a Problem of the Week is often documented and displayed in the classroom. With ample examples of strategies and procedures available, there may be times during conferences when the teacher explains what it is that the student needs to know and then uses one of these charts.

Jasmine was working to solve a percentage problem using models or drawings. During the previous week, each day the class solved a similar problem using models and drawings while working on the Calendar Board. These problem-solving processes were recorded on chart paper and displayed in the classroom. During the research phase of a conference with Jasmine, her teacher discovered that Jasmine was unclear about how to use a model or drawing for the problem she was working on. The teacher accompanied Jasmine to the charts the class had created the previous week and quickly explained the processes used. Jasmine was encouraged to use the charts as examples as she worked to solve her problem. As the conference ended, the teacher summarized the methods used and then reminded Jasmine that the charts in the classroom are there to help her when she is stumped by a problem and that mathematicians take advantage of the information they have available to them as they solve problems.

The examples to which teachers refer students may not always be class charts. Students may be encouraged to see what another student or group of students are doing. They might be guided to examples in their textbooks. They might even be asked to reread pieces of mathematics-related literature to find problem-solving strategies.

Link to the Future

Since the purpose of conferences is to give students strategies and processes that will become part of their mathematical repertoires, teachers conclude them by restating what they hope students have learned and reminding them to use these strategies in the future as they engage in mathematical tasks. By making that link to the future, students become aware of how they can take the specific learning from conferences and apply it more generally. Students often need encouragement to recognize that these ideas can be applied in other circumstances. In fact, in some cases, it helps to ask students to restate what they have learned and then to think about how they may use it in their future work. Over time, the lessons learned and then linked to future work by students strengthen the mathematical foundation upon which conceptual understanding rests.

Keeping Records of Conferences

What teachers learn as they confer with students can be as valuable as what their students learn. The focused conversational give-and-take of conferences are opportunities for teachers to gather the missing pieces of the instructional puzzle. Conferring with students gives much more comprehensive information about what students already know and what they don't yet sufficiently understand. Within the conferences themselves, some of these needs can be addressed. Moreover, teachers can use this data to tailor their instruction in the other components of the Guided Math framework. To do this effectively, teachers must have some method of recording what they learn and then use it.

There are different ways to keep records of what teachers learn from conferring. Many teachers carry clipboards upon which they have observation forms. Others record observations on sticky notes. And, others enter notes in three-ring binders or spiral notebooks.

One note-keeping form lists the standards or instructional goals for a unit. Each student is listed and the teacher can indicate whether or not each student has mastered each goal (Appendix A: Math Conference Checklist). On another form, the teacher lists the names of students as he or she confers with them and then records what was found during the research phase, what compliment he or she gave, and finally, what the teaching point was (Appendix B: Math Conference Notes 1). A third form can be used to file the sticky notes for individual students (Appendix C: Math Conference Notes 2).

Teachers have varying methods of keeping up with their notes. Three-ring binders may be used to keep these pages organized by date or by student. Some teachers prefer to use none of the forms described above. Instead, they divide spiral notebooks into sections for each of their students. When they want to record notes, they open to the appropriate section, record the date, and then note whatever they have observed.

However notes are recorded, what is most important is that they are not filed and forgotten. When used wisely, these valuable notes can guide instruction. Calkins, Hartman, and White (2005) suggests that these notes can help teachers:

- Plan for future conferences—If teachers note that many students are struggling with the same concept in a unit, they may want to confer with other students to see if they are also struggling. Or, if students seem well beyond where a teacher thought they would be, it may be worthwhile to confer with additional students to see if perhaps instruction could move ahead a little more quickly than planned originally.

- Recognize the strengths of their students—When teachers identify students who have mastered the standards being taught, they can modify the instruction for these students and allow them to move on.

- Discover future teaching options—Conference conversations suggest lessons from which students can benefit that may not be possible to address in that conference. The lessons may be ones which would benefit the whole class or a small group of students.

- Broaden the scope of conferences—As teachers review their conference notes, they may decide to confer with students based on previously noted concerns.

- Follow-up on conference teaching points—Teachers who have records of their conference teaching points with their students can follow-up on these in subsequent conferences to confirm student understanding.

Chapter Snapshot

Conferring with students during Guided Math is one of the most important components of the day. This one-on-one interaction provides teachers with information about a student's mathematical understanding as well as his or her misconceptions. Then teachers have the opportunity to challenge the student further or to correct his or her misconceptions. Conferencing can also help teachers discover when reteaching to a group of students, or the entire class, is appropriate.

In order to have the opportunity to confer individually with students on a regular basis, a strong classroom management system must be set in place. To avoid interruptions, students must understand the procedures during that time as well as what independent or group work they must complete.

It is also important for teachers to keep a record of what they learned during the conferences. There are many different systems for doing this, but when teachers find a system that works for them, they are more likely to stick with it.

Review and Reflect

1. In what ways are you able to discover your students' mathematical thinking?

2. How frequently are you able to confer with your students? If you are not able to confer as often as you would like, what prevents it?

3. What advantages are there to having structures for conferences in mind as you meet with students?

1 2 3
4 5 6
7 **8** 9

Assessment in Guided Math

Effective teaching begins with knowing about students and their mathematical knowledge. Information gathered through assessment not only provides information about where to begin instructionally, but also guides future instruction and the students' learning. The more teachers know about their students' learning during instruction, the more accurately instruction can be tailored to meet their unique needs. In addition, the more students know about the criteria for quality work and how to assess their own work against these standards, the more likely they are to strive to meet them. As the National Council of Teachers of Mathematics (2000) put it, "Assessment should not merely be done to students; rather, it should also be done for students, to guide and enhance their learning."

Ann Davies in her book *Making Classroom Assessment Work* (2000) beautifully describes assessment as being analogous to the inuksuit of the Native Americans of the North American Arctic region. Inuksuit are man-made stone markers often stacked in the shape of people and are used for navigation on the tundra. On the harsh landscape of the Arctic tundra, there are few natural landmarks, so inuksuit can make the difference between arriving safely at a destination or not arriving at all. Finding the way through instruction without direction from assessments may not be as dangerous as being lost on the tundra, but without this guidance, the effectiveness of instruction is diminished.

Assessment and evaluation have often been considered synonymous. In education, however, they have very distinct meanings. To use assessment well, teachers must be aware of these differences. Although the two serve different purposes, their roles are complementary.

During instruction, teachers are constantly gathering evidence of their students' learning—sometimes formally and sometimes informally. When this evidence of student learning is used to develop teaching practices and enhance student learning, assessment is being performed. With guidance and support, teachers want their students to learn to self-assess as they work, too. Students who engage in self-assessment begin to monitor their own learning and become better students. With assessment, a large amount of information is collected from a relatively small number of students. In essence, this process is assessment *for* learning, rather than solely *of* learning.

Evaluation, on the other hand, is the process of reviewing the evidence of student learning to decide whether students have learned what they need to know and how well they have learned it. It means judging or placing a value on student achievement. Often, for evaluations, a small amount of information is collected from a large number of students, like we see in the mandated high-stakes testing. Evaluations are frequently used as forms of accountability, for reporting student progress to others or used to identify trends (Davies 2000).

Rationales for Assessment and Evaluation

Assessment and evaluation are both essential components for learning. Unfortunately, the crucial roles they play daily in enhancing student achievement are sometimes overshadowed by the attention given to scores on the state-mandated tests. Fountas and Pinnell (1996) list the following rationales for systematic assessment:

- continually informing teaching decisions
- systematically assessing students' strengths and knowledge
- finding out what students can do, both independently and with teacher support

- documenting progress for parents and students
- summarizing achievement and learning over a given period—six weeks, a year, or longer
- reporting to administrators, school-board members, and various stakeholders in the community

These rationales focus first on the learning process in the classroom and then on the role of assessment and evaluation for accountability. The first three rationales listed on the previous page apply directly to instruction and student learning. Although informing teaching decisions is listed first, all three are interdependent and cyclical. Any of them could be said to come first, since teaching and learning are interactive processes. However, once a lesson has been taught, teachers need to find out what students know so they can plan the next instructional steps. Teachers plan, teach, assess learning, and then adjust their instruction. Eventually teachers may even be able to assess and adjust *as* they teach.

The evidence of student learning gathered by teachers is not only used to help plan instruction, it is also shared on an ongoing basis with the students and with their parents. Students improve their performances and increase their learning when they know precisely what they have done well and exactly what they need to do to improve, and then are given opportunities to do so. The assessment feedback they receive has the potential to maximize their achievement. Regular reports allow parents to monitor their children's progress. As a consequence, parents are able to provide assistance for their children at home and to reinforce their work habits. Timely, regular reports to parents also prevent unpleasant surprises when report cards go home or conferences are conducted.

Periodic summative assessments serve a more evaluative purpose. These assessments answer questions such as:

- How well did students master the curriculum?
- Are students ready to move on?
- How did the class as a whole perform?
- Does anything need to be retaught before instruction proceeds?

These evaluations are used to inform both students and their parents about their *learning*. They also give teachers an idea of how successful they have been in *teaching* the curriculum. Reflecting on the data from these evaluations helps teachers refine and focus their teaching.

School administrators and school leadership teams use the data from summative evaluations to make school-wide decisions. Teachers and administrators examine data from these assessments on a regular basis to determine how well students are learning. Rather than having to wait until the end of the year to learn how students performed, periodic performance reviews that use data from leading indicators allow teachers to fine-tune the interventions they provide for struggling students throughout the school year.

The data from high-stakes tests has enormous impact when it is used by school systems and states to determine the quality of schools. The consequences of failing to make adequate yearly progress as described by the No Child Left Behind legislation are significant and, perhaps more than any other factors, have focused the attention of educators and the population as a whole on assessment data. Student success on state-wide tests is often equated with the quality of education provided.

There has also been the widespread belief that the consistent monitoring of learning through standardized testing would intensify and hasten school improvement. Unfortunately, this belief ignores the dual consequences of the extensive use of mandated standardized testing. *Some* students who have experienced success in learning will redouble their efforts and achieve more than they would have otherwise. *Other* students who have experienced repeated academic failure simply give up in hopelessness. As Stiggins (2002) describes it, "Some come to slay the dragon, while others expect to be devoured by it. As a result, high-stakes testing will enhance the learning of some, while discouraging others and causing them to give up."

Without effective use of assessment within classrooms to enhance student achievement, we may actually hinder the success of the very students that we hope to motivate to succeed. It is vital to remember that teachers, although they may have little say in the state-mandated tests, can determine the kinds of assessments used in their classrooms and the way in which those assessments are used to promote learning.

Assessment and Learning in Guided Math

Ongoing assessment *for* learning is essential to inform instruction, especially during Guided Math. Without a sound understanding of assessment and how to use it to adjust teaching, teachers find it difficult to successfully guide mathematics instruction. The specificity of information derived from formative assessments is crucial in steering teachers as they make day-to-day instructional decisions. Therefore, teachers must not only assess more frequently, but also manage the assessment data effectively. By accumulating, summarizing, analyzing, and reporting assessment results efficiently, teachers have in hand the information they need to make instructional decisions more effectively (Stiggins 2005).

A Vision for Learning

When beginning a task, most people, young or old, want to know precisely what needs to be done to be successful. Young artists hone their skills by trying to reproduce masterpieces. Musicians listen to the works of virtuosos. In fact, people tend to be more successful in any endeavor if they have in mind a vision of success for which to aim. When teachers give their students an idea of what success "looks" like, these students, too, have a much better chance of attaining it. This is especially true with students who lack the experience and background knowledge needed to construct their own visions.

When planning a unit of study, teachers need to closely examine the standards, identify what students need to learn, and determine how to assess and evaluate students' learning. Unfortunately, those expectations are not always shared with students. While some students seem to easily figure out what is needed to be successful, students who most often struggle with learning are frequently the students who also have trouble knowing the expectations. Students who are made aware of these expectations find it easier to identify important concepts during instruction and to monitor their own learning.

Davies (2000) lists three steps for teachers in the process of linking descriptions of expectations to instruction:

1. *Describe what students need to learn in a language that students and parents will understand.* Summarize learning goals in clear, simple language. This is a more difficult process than it may seem. The goal is a strong alignment of the student-friendly language of the learning expectations with the standards themselves.

2. *Share the description with students and explain how it relates to success in life outside of school.* As a unit of study begins, students should be given a description of what they need to learn and an opportunity to discuss exactly what it entails. When the descriptions are accompanied by samples of what success looks like, students begin to be able to monitor their learning. If students are shown a set of samples or exemplars that illustrate what development looks like over time, the learning destination becomes more clear. The exemplars can be used to help develop criteria for success with students, show ways students can represent their learning, assess and provide descriptive feedback, and help parents understand learning expectations.

3. *Use the description to guide instruction, assessment, and evaluation.* Since the descriptions are aligned directly to the standards, instruction should directly address the descriptions. Throughout the unit, the assessment and evaluations will be based on the evidence of success described. If they know exactly what the learning expectations are, assessments and evaluations should cause no surprises for students.

Establishing Criteria for Success with Checklists and Rubrics

Teachers cannot assess student learning without having in mind clearly established criteria for success. The criteria are developed by carefully examining the standards being learned to understand what should be construed as evidence of success. How will students show how well they know or can do what the standards specify? In the past, teachers relied almost solely on assessments created by textbook companies or else created assessments themselves once they had finished teaching a unit. Frequently, the teacher-created assessments were based on what had been taught, rather than directly on the curriculum.

With today's emphasis on standards-based learning, teachers now determine how they will assess student learning by focusing on the standards before planning for instruction. When they have determined how to assess their students, many teachers develop specific criteria for success from which they create checklists or rubrics. A checklist or rubric not only provides a basis for a final evaluation of student work, but is also used for formative assessment and for student self-assessment, enabling students to revisit and revise their work before it is graded.

To help students fully understand the criteria for quality work, teachers often involve them in the process of creating the assessment checklists and rubrics. By providing a series of work samples showing how student learning progresses over time and discussing the merits of these exemplars with their classes, teachers help their students discover what is required to meet the standard. Students, with teacher guidance, determine and list the criteria, which will be used later to assess their work. The criteria can be the basis from which to create checklists or rubrics that can be used by teachers to assess work products of students. The checklists or rubrics can also be used to help students monitor their own progress. Additionally, students can use these assessment tools as they conference with their peers. In fact, when students engage in peer conferences, they gain a better understanding of the criteria and have opportunities to hone their mathematical communication skills.

The criteria also serves as the basis for specific descriptive feedback, which teachers share with their students, letting them know specifically what it is that they have done well and what needs further work. This feedback allows students to improve the quality of their work using the comments they receive.

Using Checklists

Figure 8.1 provides an example of criteria for problem solving. Although there are criteria listed, the checklist itself does not describe specifically what would be required to be considered proficient or exemplary in each criterion. Even though a checklist may be more easily created than a rubric, it may not be as effective when used with students, unless the teacher provides a significant amount of very specific feedback supporting students as they strive to improve their work. The checklist has a column to check if students have met the criteria and another column labeled "Not Yet Met," which clearly communicates to students that more work is expected in order to meet the criteria. After the checklist has been completed for a piece of student work, the student is then given an opportunity to revise his or her work so that it meets the criteria.

Figure 8.1 Problem-Solving Checklist

Criteria for Problem-Solving Checklist	Met	Not Yet Met	Comments
1. Mathematical representations of the problem were appropriate.			
2. An appropriate strategy was used to solve the problem.			
3. Computation was accurate.			
4. The problem-solving process was clearly explained.			
5. Problem solving was extended through recognition of patterns, relationships, or connections to other areas of mathematics or to real-life applications.			

Checklists give students criteria without distinguishing levels of quality. So, checklists indicate whether students have met specific criteria in their work product, but they do not necessarily measure how well they have met the criteria. As they assess students' work, teachers, peers, or students themselves should add comments regarding the quality of the students' work for each criterion, letting students know how well they met it and focusing on ways to improve.

Using Rubrics

In contrast to a checklist of criteria, a rubric is a scoring guide that sets forth precise levels of quality for each criterion. (See Figure 8.2 on the following page.) Rubrics usually list several criteria or domains and then specify gradations of proficiency for each criterion. Sometimes, a scale is included, which allows teachers to determine a numerical grade using the rubric. Because it is much more specific, it is easier for students to use to identify precisely how to make improvements in their work. When rubrics are developed with student input, they are often most effective because students understand them more thoroughly. They become tools for reflection and peer review.

Rubrics that are developed to be used with multiple tasks or assignments allow students to become familiar with the criteria and the levels of proficiency described. They should be available to students before they begin their work and should be posted in the classroom for reference by teachers and students, whenever applicable. Teachers should introduce rubrics by modeling their use with an exemplar, thinking aloud as they rate the quality of the work. Later students, working together and lead by teachers, can assess other exemplars using the same rubric. By having the process modeled first and then being involved in a group effort using a rubric to assess work, students learn how to use this form of assessment. Not only will they understand the assessment process when their teachers assess their work using a rubric, but they will also be able to assess their peers' work and self-assess their own work more effectively.

Criteria for Problem-Solving Rubric

Figure 8.2 Criteria for Problem-Solving Rubric

Domain	Emerging	Developing	Proficient	Exemplary
Conceptual Understanding	Mathematical representations of the problem were incorrect. The wrong information was used. Procedures used would not solve the problem.	Mathematical representation was inefficient or inaccurate. Some, but not all, of the relevant information was used. Procedures used would lead to a partially correct solution.	Mathematical representation was appropriate. All the relevant information was used. Procedures used would lead to a correct solution.	Mathematical representations helped clarify the problem's meaning. Inferred or hidden information was used. Procedures used would lead to concise and efficient solution.
Reasoning	Strategies used were not appropriate. Reasoning did not support the work. Logic was not apparent.	Oversimplified strategies were used to solve the problem. Little reasoning was offered that justified the work. Leaps in logic were hard to follow.	Appropriate strategies were used to solve the problem. Each step was justified. Logic of solution was obvious.	Innovative, creative strategies were used to solve the problem. Solution was proved to be correct. Examples and counterexamples were given to support the logic of solution.
Computation and Execution	Serious errors in computation led to incorrect solution. Representations were seriously flawed. No evidence was given of how answer was computed.	Minor computational errors were made. Representations were mostly correct, but not accurately labeled. Evidence for solutions was inconsistent or unclear.	Computation was accurate. Representations were complete and accurate. Work clearly supported the solution.	All aspects of the solution were accurate. Multiple representations verified the solution. Multiple ways to compute the answer were shown.

Domain	Emerging	Developing	Proficient	Exemplary
Communication	Little or no explanation for the work was given. Mathematical vocabulary was incorrect.	Explanation was not clearly stated. Mathematical vocabulary was used imprecisely.	Explanation was easy to follow. Mathematical vocabulary was used correctly.	Explanation was clear and concise. Mathematical vocabulary was used precisely.
Connections	Unable to recognize patterns and relationships. Found no connections to other disciplines or real-life applications.	Recognized some patterns and relationships. Found a hint of connections to other disciplines or real-life applications.	Recognized important patterns and relationships. Connection was made to other disciplines or real-life applications.	A general rule or formula for solving related problems was created. Connection to other disciplines or real-life applications was accurate and realistic.

Adapted from a rubric created by the Mathematics and Science Education Center of the Northwest Regional Educational Laboratory (http://www.nwrel.org/msec/images/mpm/pdf/scoregrid.pdf)

When rubrics are well aligned with the mathematical standards, they are not just about evaluating a student's work, they are about teaching. Rubrics focus our instruction as we teach. They help students understand the goals of their assignments so they can focus their efforts. And finally, they allow teachers to provide critiques of student work that are individualized and constructive in a timely manner (Andrade 2005).

The Value of Descriptive Feedback

Research shows that one of the most effective instructional strategies that teachers employ is providing students specific descriptive feedback. This lets students know how well they are doing relative to the learning objectives (Marzano, Pickering, and Pollock 2001; Hattie 1992). According to the National Council of Teachers of Mathematics (2000), feedback supports "students in setting goals, assuming responsibility for their own learning and becoming more independent learners." Additionally, feedback helps them understand exactly what is required for complete and correct responses. When feedback is guidance specific to learning targets, this assessment *for* learning scaffolds students as they work "to close the gap between where they are now and where we want them to be" (Stiggins 2005).

Many people are used to receiving feedback. Athletes are coached as they train. Coaches give specific feedback with the goal of maximizing their performance. The coaching is not given only at the end of an event, but instead, is given during training so that the athletes are able to make adjustments to improve their performances prior to testing them in competitions. Similarly, teachers who provide feedback to their students during their work, rather than after it has been completed, help their students maximize their learning.

Teachers need to tell students about their learning—both what they are doing well and what needs improvement. Students then use the feedback to adjust what they are doing. According to Ann Davies (2000), descriptive feedback:

- comes during and after the learning
- is easily understood
- is related directly to the learning
- is specific, so performance can improve
- involves choice on the part of the learner as to the type of feedback and how to receive it
- is part of an ongoing conversation about learning
- is in comparison to models, exemplars, samples, or descriptions
- is about the performance or the work—not the person

Marzano, Pickering, and Pollock (2001) examined numerous studies on the effects of providing feedback and drew the following generalizations to guide its use:

1. *Feedback should be "corrective" in nature.* Feedback that only tells students that their answers are correct or incorrect actually has a negative impact on achievement, while significant positive effects were reported when the feedback lets students know *what* it is they are doing that is correct or incorrect. Furthermore, when students are asked to continue to work on a task until they are successful, achievement is enhanced.

2. *Feedback should be timely.* Timeliness appears to be critical to the effectiveness of feedback. Generally, the greater the delay in receiving feedback, the less improvement there will be in achievement.

3. *Feedback should be specific to criterion.* By linking feedback to the criteria for success that have been established, students have guidance as to how they can improve their achievement. In contrast, when feedback is normative in nature, they only know how they did in comparison to the performance of other students. They are often at a loss as to how they can improve what they are doing. Likewise, when the feedback students receive is only a percentage score, students may be motivated to improve it, but may not know how to be more successful. Feedback based on checklists and rubrics which provide the criteria necessary for a quality performance foster improved student achievement.

4. *Students can effectively provide some of their own feedback.* When students are aware of the expectations for work products or performance, they can track their achievement as learning occurs. The release of responsibility to students encourages them to become more cognizant of the quality of their work as they monitor it relative to the established criteria.

Involving Students in the Assessment Process

Fosnot and Dolk (2001) eloquently describe what makes student involvement in the assessment process so valuable with this quote, "When young mathematicians are hard at work, they are thinking, they become puzzled, they become intrigued; they are learning to see their world through a mathematical lens. Assessment needs to capture the view this lens reveals."

What teachers learn about students from their work products has its limitations. The ultimate evidence of learning comes from within our young learners. What exactly do they know, perceive, infer, and understand? Without access to glimpses of the world through their own unique mathematical lenses, we may be blind to some of their achievements or to some of their needs. The closest we can come to fully understanding their mathematical perspectives is through involving our students in self-assessment.

Students becoming more involved in assessing their own learning not only offers teachers a more complete vision of the students' achievements, but also enhances those achievements. Students shift from being passively involved to becoming more active participants. According to Davies (2000), students who are involved in shaping and assessing their own learning are more likely to:

- understand what is expected of them
- access prior knowledge
- have some ownership over making it happen
- be able to give themselves descriptive feedback as they are learning
- give the information teachers need to adjust their teaching

Students who develop more metacognitive awareness of their own mathematical learning begin to tap into their prior experiences and background knowledge to make connections that strengthen their understanding. Becoming more conscious of the *how* of learning, they are motivated to assume greater responsibility for their own learning. By assessing their own achievements by using criteria from checklists or rubrics and then communicating evidence of their learning to their teachers, students essentially reveal views of the world as seen through their own mathematical lenses. These glimpses of the mathematical perspectives of students provide insights which allow teachers to more effectively meet the individual learning needs of their students. Self-assessment by students, far from being a luxury, is an essential component of formative assessment (Black and William 1998).

Closely associated with self-assessment is allowing students to engage in setting their own goals. Once students have become more aware of the learning process itself, what they need to learn, and where they are in the learning trajectory, teachers can help their students set goals for their next learning steps. Setting individual goals increases student motivation since these goals have value for them (Madden 1997). Students learn what it means to be in charge of their own learning—to monitor their own successes and make decisions about how to maximize their achievements (Stiggins 2002).

Formative Assessment

Formative assessment is intrinsically assessment *for* learning. It is a systematic process to continuously gather evidence about individual and class learning so that instruction can be adapted to enhance student achievement. Formative assessment and teaching are complementary processes, one supporting the other. Studies show that formative assessment helps low-achieving students more than other students, thus reducing the range of achievement and raising achievement overall (Black and William 1998).

Teachers use formative assessments and the information obtained from them to advance rather than just check on student learning. According to Stiggins (2002), teachers do this by:

- understanding and articulating in advance of teaching the achievement targets that their students are to hit

- informing their students about those learning goals, in terms that students understand, from the very beginning of the teaching and learning process

- becoming assessment literate and thus able to transform their expectations into assessment exercises and scoring procedures that accurately reflect student achievement

- using classroom assessments to build students' confidence in themselves as learners and help them take responsibility for their own learning, in order to lay foundations for lifelong learning

- translating classroom-assessment results into frequent descriptive feedback (versus judgmental feedback) for students, providing them with specific insights as to how to improve

- engaging students in regular self-assessment, with standards held constant so that students can watch themselves grow over time and thus feel in charge of their own success

- actively involving students in communicating with their teachers and their families about their achievement status and improvement.

Teachers who engage in formative assessment in their classrooms must not only understand how they can assess on an ongoing basis so that they are aware of individual student achievements and needs, but also how they can manage their classroom so that they can indeed use the assessment information they have to meet the instructional needs they have identified. With traditional modes of instruction, this is difficult to do. When teachers implement Guided Math in their classrooms, they have a model that allows them to group students flexibly to effectively address the identified instructional next steps for students.

Assessments for Guided Math Groups

Teachers who use Guided Reading in their classrooms know that students are grouped according to their reading levels. These levels are determined by administering running records. Using the results of the running records, an instructional reading level is determined for each student. This is a level that is not too easy, but not so hard that it would be frustrating for the student to try to read. The instructional level is one at which, with a little support from the teacher, a student can read successfully. With practice, that level will become too easy and the instructional level will be raised.

Unfortunately, for mathematics instruction, there is no comparable assessment. Teachers use a number of means of grouping students for Guided Math. Some teachers use pretests for initial grouping when beginning a new unit. Throughout the unit, they may give brief formative assessments to monitor learning and then adjust the grouping, as needed. Some teachers create checklists of knowledge and skills based on instructional standards. Informal observations of student work and conferences with students may also help teachers create or modify groups based on levels of student learning. Additionally, some computerized programs offer prescriptive assessment data.

The goal of grouping in Guided Math, however, is similar to that of Guided Reading. Students should work at an "instructional" level that is just right for them—not too easy, but not so hard that it frustrates them. Ideally, the instruction during small-group work allows students to stretch their understanding with support from the teacher and then practice at that level until they become proficient. If some students in the group become proficient before the others, they are moved out of the group.

Some groups may remain constant for several weeks. Some may meet for several weeks, but the composition of the group may change during that time. Other groups may meet just once or twice to work on a specific targeted area of instruction. The utility of the Guided Math framework is that it provides for such flexibility.

What is essential and is a distinguishing characteristic of Guided Math classrooms, though, is the use of assessment *for* learning. Assessment in Guided Math classrooms is ongoing and informs instructional decisions. The strong links between teaching, learning, and assessment are evident. Although evaluation certainly has a role in these classrooms, it is not a substitute for the consistent and pervasive use of formative assessment. Formative assessment is the determining factor in creating groups and, then in planning lessons for each group. So, despite the fact that assessment is discussed in chapter eight, rather late in this book, assessment *for* learning is a defining characteristic of Guided Math.

Chapter Snapshot

Assessment is more than testing—it is evaluating students' progress, their understandings and misconceptions, their ability to solve problems and think critically, and their ability to apply their knowledge to new situations. Information from assessments should be used to tailor instruction to meet the learning needs of the students. Assessment not only keeps students accountable, it keeps teachers accountable.

Depending on the type of information that is desired, formative or summative assessments can be used. Formative assessments should be given throughout a unit of study as a way to monitor progress. Summative assessments should be given at the end of a unit to gauge total comprehension of a concept. Rubrics and checklists are two methods of assessment that allow for teacher and student evaluation and can be used as a formative or summative assessment. Regardless of the type of assessment, it is important for students to receive feedback on their progress that is both constructive and timely. With teacher discussions, students can learn to use this feedback and apply it to future learning.

Review and Reflect

1. Why is assessment essential in a Guided Math classroom? What role does it play in teaching and in learning?

2. What kinds of assessments do you use in your classroom? Is there a blend of assessments and evaluations?

Putting It Into Practice

The students who enter our classrooms at the beginning of each school year seldom think of themselves as mathematicians. They often consider mathematics to be a set of rules dispensed by teachers and then memorized for tests. Rarely are they aware of mathematical connections to their daily lives, now or in the future. Mathematics is not seen as a system of relationships and patterns that have been discovered by people as they pondered their mathematical observations. Nor is it considered a subject of wonder and puzzlement. Most students have a very narrow view of the subject.

As we seek to add rigor and relevance to our mathematical instruction, we hope to involve our students in learning experiences that move them beyond this limited view, stimulating their curiosity about math, to open their eyes to the mathematical musings that lead mathematicians to extol on the beauty of the discipline. Students who are given opportunities to explore, solve problems, and generate conjectures are truly acting as young mathematicians. They learn to appreciate the value of mathematics. It is difficult to envision this kind of learning with the traditional mode of teaching.

The desire to inspire students and to meet their diverse needs is what motivates teachers to continuously reflect on their teaching practices and adapt them. The Guided Math framework offers teachers an alternative to the standard whole-class instructional model so frequently used for mathematics instruction. Because Guided Math provides a flexible model of classroom instruction, teachers have the option of planning a variety of mathematics lessons that not only target specific instructional needs, but also allow students to participate in investigations and problem-solving activities that stimulate their curiosity, lead them to discover patterns and relationships, and link these mathematical concepts to real-world applications.

To implement Guided Math in the classroom, it is important to keep in mind what helps students as they become young mathematicians. Ideally, students who are learning mathematics should:

- enjoy exploring problem solving in a risk-free environment where errors are seen as learning opportunities
- have chances to try out strategies on a variety of challenging problems
- learn to identify appropriate strategies to use when problem solving
- feel the satisfaction of struggling with difficult problems and then finally solving them
- receive specific feedback from teachers and peers on their mathematical work
- participate in mathematical conversations using mathematical vocabulary and justifying their work
- expand their mathematical understanding through problem-solving tasks and mathematical discourse
- learn to recognize patterns and relationships leading to the development of conjectures
- make mathematical connections

Given these opportunities, students learn that thinking mathematically makes sense. Moreover, they come to believe that *they* are capable of making sense of mathematics (Van de Walle and Lovin 2006).

Of course, there is no one simple method for teaching mathematics effectively. It is a complex process. However, teachers who understand and teach the mathematics standards, use ongoing assessment to guide their instruction, lead their students to construct broader mathematical meaning from their specific mathematical tasks, and create a community of learners where mathematics communication is the norm nurture and develop the conceptual understanding of their students.

In *Comprehending Math: Adapting Reading Strategies to Teach Mathematics K–6*, Hyde (2006) describes how thinking, language, and mathematics can be braided together into a "tightly knit entity like a rope that is stronger than the individual strands." Just as reading is closely linked to thinking and language, so is mathematics. The three components are inseparable, mutually supportive, and necessary. In reading, students can use the discrete decoding skills they have learned, and construct meaning by interacting with the text. They draw upon their background knowledge, infer, make connections, ask questions, visualize, determine importance, and synthesize, combining the new information with the old to construct meaning. In working with mathematics, students need to be encouraged to use the same strategies as they construct mathematical meaning.

Expanding on the similarities between reading-comprehension strategies and mathematics-comprehension strategies, Hyde goes on to list these questions he adapted from reading strategies for teachers of mathematics to consider:

1. Are students expected to *construct their own meaning* in mathematics?

2. Are students encouraged to have *ownership of their problem solving*—to choose to use mathematics for purposes they set for themselves?

3. Are students encouraged to do problem solving for *authentic purposes*?

4. Are students encouraged to do *voluntary mathematics*, selecting tasks for information, pleasure, or to fulfill personal goals?

5. How is mathematics instruction *scaffolded*?

6. Does the school help teachers and students build a *rich, mathematically literate environment* or community?

7. Are students encouraged to see the *big picture, important concepts, and vital connections* versus isolated pieces of mathematics?

8. Is *forgiveness* granted to students in mathematics? Is *making mistakes a natural* part of learning? Is doing mathematics seen as a dynamic process that incorporates *planning, drafting, revising, editing, and publishing*?

These are worth considering as teachers implement Guided Math in their classrooms. The word *teachers* is plural because it helps to have support during a time of change. If teachers join together to form learning communities as they refine their instructional practices, the process is often much easier and more effective. Working together, teachers examine and then reflect on their teaching practices. They plan, teach, reflect, share, and refine. This ongoing collaboration leads to growth in the teaching dynamics of the entire group.

Lyons and Pinnell (2001) write that teachers learn best when they are actively participating with a group of their peers and are in a respected learning community. They have opportunities to observe each other as they try out new concepts. Because they share the responsibility for their learning, they are able to freely discuss common concerns. They feel safe and supported as they try out new teaching strategies.

These learning communities do not have to be part of the organized staff development that is required. Groups of teachers who share an interest in exploring ways to meet the diverse mathematical needs of their students can work together voluntarily. In fact, those groups are usually some of the most successful because these teachers begin the process with the desire to work together and learn. These groups might meet before or after school, during common planning periods, during planning times supported by the school administration when substitute teachers are hired or during other regular time that is arranged through creative scheduling.

As we share and learn together as professionals, we need to maintain our focus on our students. Regie Routman (2003) wisely writes,

"When I suggest that we need to 'teach with a sense of urgency,' I'm not talking about teaching prompted by anxiety but rather about making every moment in the classroom count, about ensuring that our instruction engages students and moves them ahead, about using daily evaluation and reflection to make wise teaching decisions. Complacency will not get our students where they need to be. I am relaxed and happy when I am working with students, but I am also mindful of where I need to get them and how little time I have in which to do it. I teach each day with a sense of urgency. Specifically, that means that I am very aware of the students in front of me, the opportunities for teaching and evaluating on the spot, the skills and strategies I need to be teaching, the materials I need, the amount of time available and the optimal contexts and curriculum."

As hurried and harried as teachers can become, they must keep their students and their students' learning needs in mind. Sometimes, to do this, teachers simply need to slow down so they can teach more deeply. Teaching within an effective instructional framework, with a clear focus, and an intimate knowledge of the students' learning needs, a teacher can actually "do more instruction, more effectively, in less time" (Routman 2003). And, all the while, teachers must do what they can to make learning a joyful enterprise for their students.

A large part of what makes learning a joyful experience for students is the relationship they have with their teachers. Building a personal connection with students is at the heart of teaching; students need to know teachers respect them and care about them. When teachers slow down, they can listen to their students, be sure their students have opportunities for success, and then celebrate those successes with their students. Teachers show students that their unique qualities are valued. Only when these relationships are built are students willing to take the risks necessary for profound learning, whether in mathematics or any other subject area.

The Guided Math framework described throughout this book is a structure upon which teachers can build their mathematics instruction along with their students. It is based on research, experience from the classroom, and collaboration and conversation with other educators. In spite of that, only when individual teachers use it in their classrooms is it fully fleshed out. The teaching styles of individual teachers, the curriculum they are teaching, and their students' unique strengths and needs determine the features of the framework once it has evolved and is implemented in classrooms.

Teachers considering the Guided Math framework should reflect on how they can adapt and use it to inspire a love of learning in their students, promote their students' deep conceptual understanding of the mathematical standards, and establish a vibrant learning community within their classes. It takes devoted teachers to individualize the framework and turn it into the mainstay of their mathematics instruction.

Review and Reflect

1. How will you begin to implement the Guided Math framework in your classroom?

2. How can you create a professional learning community to support you as you modify your mathematics instruction?

Math Conference Checklist

Student Names   **Math Goals**

Appendix **B**

Math Conference Notes 1

Student	Date	Research	Compliment	Teaching Point

Math Conference Notes 2

Appendix D

Criteria for Problem-Solving Rubric

Domain	Conceptual Understanding	Reasoning
Emerging	Mathematical representations of the problem were incorrect. The wrong information was used. Procedures used would not solve the problem.	Strategies used were not appropriate. Reasoning did not support the work. Logic was not apparent.
Developing	Mathematical representation was inefficient or inaccurate. Some, but not all, of the relevant information was used. Procedures used would lead to a partially correct solution.	Oversimplified strategies were used to solve the problem. Little reasoning was offered that justified the work. Leaps in logic were hard to follow.
Proficient	Mathematical representation was appropriate. All the relevant information was used. Procedures used would lead to a correct solution.	Appropriate strategies were used to solve the problem. Each step was justified. Logic of the solution was obvious.
Exemplary	Mathematical representations helped clarify the problem's meaning. Inferred or hidden information was used. Procedures used would lead to a concise and efficient solution.	Innovative, creative strategies were used to solve the problem. The solution was proved correct. Examples and counterexamples were given to support the logic of the solution.

Computation and Execution	Connections	Communication
Serious errors in computation led to an incorrect solution. Representations were seriously flawed. No evidence was given of how the answer was computed.	Unable to recognize patterns and relationships. Found no connections to other disciplines or real-life applications.	Little or no explanation for the work was given. Mathematical vocabulary was incorrect.
Minor computational errors were made. Representations were mostly correct, but not accurately labeled. Evidence for solutions was inconsistent or unclear.	Recognized some patterns and relationships. Found a hint of connections to other disciplines or real-life applications.	Explanation was not clearly stated. Mathematical vocabulary was used imprecisely.
Computation was accurate. Representations were complete and accurate. Work clearly supported the solution.	Recognized important patterns and relationships. Connection was made to other disciplines or real-life applications.	Explanation was easy to follow. Mathematical vocabulary was used correctly.
All aspects of the solution were accurate. Multiple representations verified the solution. Multiple ways to compute the answer were shown.	A general rule or formula for solving related problems was created. Connection to other disciplines or real-life applications was accurate and realistic.	Explanation was clear and concise. Mathematical vocabulary was used precisely.

Adapted from a rubric created by the Northwest Regional Educational Laboratory (http://www.nwrel.org/msec/images/mpm/pdf/scoregrid.pdf)

Appendix E

Problem-Solving Checklist

Criteria for Problem Solving	Met	Not Yet Met	Comments
1. Mathematical representations of the problem were appropriate.			
2. An appropriate strategy was used to solve the problem.			
3. Computation was accurate.			
4. The problem solving process was clearly explained.			
5. Problem solving was extended through recognition of patterns, relationships, or connections to other areas of mathematics or to real-life applications.			

Name: _____ Date: _____

Task: _____

Assessed by: _____ Self   _____ Peer   _____ Teacher

References Cited

Andrade, H. G. 2005. Teaching with rubrics: The good, the bad, and the ugly. *College Teaching.* 53(1): 27.

Bamberger, H. J., and C. Oberdorf. 2007. *Introduction to connections.* The Math Process Standards Series. Portsmouth, NH: Heinemann.

Barrata-Lorton, M. 1976. *Mathematics their way.* Menlo Park, CA: Addison-Wesley Publishing Company.

Black, P., and D. William. 1998. Inside the black box: Raising standards through classroom assessment. *Phi Delta Kappa.* 80.

Burns, M. 2000. *About teaching mathematics: A K–8 resource.* Sausalito, CA: Math Solutions Publication.

Calkins, L. 1994. *The art of teaching writing.* Portsmouth, NH: Heinemann.

———. 2000. *The art of teaching reading.* Boston, MA: Allyn and Bacon.

Calkins, L., A. Hartman, and Z. White. 2005. *One to one: The art of conferring with young writers.* Portsmouth, NH: Heinemann.

Cambourne, B. 1988. *The whole story: Natural learning and the acquisition of literacy in the classroom.* New York, NY: Ashton Scholastic.

Carpenter, T., M. Franke, and L. Levi. 2003. *Thinking mathematically: Integrating arithmetic and algebra in elementary school.* Portsmouth, NH: Heinemann.

Cochran, L. 1991. The art of the universe. *Journal of Mathematical Behavior* 10: 213–214. Quoted in Van de Walle and Lovin 2006, ix.

Collins, K. 2004. *Growing readers: Units of study in the primary classroom.* York, ME: Stenhouse.

Davies, A. 2000. *Making classroom assessment work.* Courtenay, Canada: Connections Publishing.

Devlin, K. 2005. *The math instinct.* New York, NY: Thunder's Mouth Press.

Ennis, B. H., and K. S. Witeck. 2007. *Introduction to representation.* The Math Process Standards Series. Portsmouth, NH: Heinemann.

Franke, M. L., C. P. Carpenter, L. Levi, and E. Fennema. 2001. Capturing teachers' generative change: A follow-up study of professional development in mathematics. *American Educational Research Journal.* 38: 654–689.

Fletcher, R., and J. Portalupi. 2001. *Writing workshop: The essential guide.* Portsmouth, NH: Heinemann.

Fosnot, C., and M. Dolk. 2001. *Young mathematicians at work: Constructing number sense, addition, and subtraction.* Portsmouth, NH: Heinemann.

Fountas, I., and G. Pinnell. 1996. *Guided reading: Good first teaching for all children.* Portsmouth, NH: Heinemann.

———. 2001. *Guiding readers and writers grades 3–6.* Portsmouth, NH: Heinemann.

Gillespie, J. G., and P. F. Kanter. 2005. *Every day counts calendar math: Grade 3 teacher's guide.* Wilmington, MA: Great Source Education Group.

Harvey, S., and A. Goudvis. 2000. *Strategies that work: Teaching comprehension to enhance understanding.* York, ME: Stenhouse.

Hattie, J. A. 1992. Measuring the effects of schooling. *Australian Journal of Education* 36 (1): 5–13. Quoted in R. Marzano, D. Pickering, and J. Pollock, *Classroom instruction that works* (Alexandria, VA: Association for Supervision and Curriculum Development, 2001), 96.

Hiebert, J., and T. P. Carpenter. 1992. Learning and teaching with understanding. In Grouws (Ed.) *Handbook of research in mathematics teaching and learning.* New York: Macmillan.

Hiebert, J., T. P. Carpenter, E. Fennema, K. Fuson, D. Wearne, H. Murray, A. Oliver, and P. Human. 1997. *Making sense: Teaching and learning mathematics with understanding.* Portsmouth, NH: Heinemann.

Hoyt, L. 2002. *Make it real: Strategies for success with informational texts.* Portsmouth, NH: Heinemann.

Hyde, A. 2006. *Comprehending math: Adapting reading strategies to teach mathematics, K–6.* Portsmouth, NH: Heinemann.

Keene, E. O., and S. Zimmermann. 1997. *Mosaic of thought: Teaching comprehension in a readers' workshop.* Portsmouth, NH: Heinemann.

Lyons, C. A., and G. S. Pinnell. 2001. *Systems for change in literacy education: A guide to professional development.* Portsmouth, NH: Heinemann.

Madden, L. E. 1997. Motivating students to learn better through own goal-setting. *Education.* 117 (3): 411.

Marzano, R. J. 2004. *Building background knowledge for academic achievement: Research on what works in schools.* Alexandria, VA: Association for Supervision and Curriculum Development.

Marzano, R. J., and D. J. Pickering. 2005. *Building academic vocabulary: Teacher's manual.* Alexandria, VA: Association for Supervision and Curriculum Development.

Marzano, R. J., D. J. Pickering, and J. E. Pollock. 2001. *Classroom instruction that works*. Alexandria, VA: Association for Supervision and Curriculum Development.

Mathematics and Science Education Center. *Mathematics problem solving scoring guide*. Northwest Regional Educational Laboratory. http://www.nwrel.org/msec/images/mpm/pdf/scoregrid.pdf.

Miller, D. 2002. *Reading with meaning: Teaching comprehension in the primary grades*. Portland, ME: Stenhouse.

———. 2008. *Teaching with intention: Defining beliefs, aligning practice, taking action*. Portland, ME: Stenhouse.

Myhill, D., S. Jones, and R. Hopper. 2006. *Talking, listening, learning: Effective talk in the primary classroom*. Maidenhead, England: Open University Press.

National Center for Education Statistics. Institute of Education Sciences. U.S. Department of Education. *The nation's report card, long-term trends 2004*. http://nces.ed.gov/nationsreportcard/ltt/result 004/ (accessed July 1, 2008).

National Council of Teachers of Mathematics (NCTM). 2000. *Principles and standards for school mathematics*. Reston, VA: National Council of Teachers of Mathematics.

Nichols, M. 2006. *Comprehension through conversation: The power of purposeful talk in the reading workshop*. Portsmouth, NH: Heinemann.

O'Connell, S. 2007a. *Introduction to communication*. The Math Process Standards Series. Portsmouth, NH: Heinemann.

———. 2007b. *Introduction to problem solving*. The Math Process Standards Series. Portsmouth, NH: Heinemann.

Owocki, G. 2003. *Comprehension: Strategic instruction for K–3 students*. Portsmouth, NH: Heinemann.

Pearson, P., and M. Gallagher. 1983. The instruction of reading comprehension. *Contemporary Educational Psychology* 8: 317–344.

Phillips, G. 2007. *Chance favors the prepared mind: Mathematics and science indicators for comparing states and nations.* Washington, DC: American Institute for Research. http://www.air.org/publications/documents/Phillips.chance.favors.the.prepared.mind.pdf .

Routman, R. 2003. *Reading essential: The specifics you need to teach reading well.* Portsmouth, NH: Heinemann.

Schultz-Ferrell, K., B. Hammond, and J. Robles. 2007. *Introduction to reasoning and proof.* The Math Process Standards Series. Portsmouth, NH: Heinemann.

Scieszka, J., and Smith, L. 1995. *Math curse.* New York, NY: Viking.

Steele, D. 1999. Learning mathematical language in the zone of proximal development. *Teaching Children Mathematics* 6 (1): 38.

Stiggins, R. 2002. Assessment crisis: The absence of assessment for learning—if we wish to maximize student achievement in the U.S., we must pay far greater attention to the improvement of classroom assessment. *Phi Delta Kappan* 83 (10): 758.

———. 2004. New Assessment Beliefs for a New School Mission. *Phi Delta Kappan* 86 (1): 22.

———. 2005. From formative assessment to assessment for learning: A path to success in standards-based schools. *Phi Delta Kappan* 87 (4): 324.

Taylor-Cox, J. 2008. *Differentiating in Number & Operations and Other Math Content Standards.* Portsmouth, NH: Heinemann

Thompson, M., and J. Thompson. 2005. *Learning-focused schools strategies notebook.* Boone, NC: Learning Concepts Inc.

Tomlinson, C. A. 2000. Reconcilable differences? Standards-based teaching and differentiation. *Educational Leadership* 58 (September): 6–11.

U.S. Department of Education. 2008. *The final report of the National Mathematics Advisory Panel.* Report of the National Mathematics Advisory Panel.

Van de Walle, J., and L. Lovin. 2006. *Teaching student-centered mathematics,* 2 vols. Boston, MA: Pearson.

Viorst, J. 1988. *Alexander who used to be rich last Sunday.* New York, NY: Simon and Schuster.

Vygotsky, L.S. 1978. *Mind in society: The development of higher psychological processes.* Cambridge, MA: Harvard University Press.

Whitin, P., and D. J. Whitin. 2000. *Math is language too.* Urbana, IL: National Council of Teachers of English and Reston, VA: National Council of Teachers of Mathematics.

Zike, D. 2003. *Big book of math: Read, write, research.* San Antonio, TX: Dinah-Might Adventures.